VILLAGE WITCH

*This book is dedicated to the Old Ones
and in loving memory of Mab*

VILLAGE WITCH

by

Cassandra Latham-Jones

Acknowledgements

Grateful thanks to the following people for their input
and advice:

Laetitia Latham-Jones, Angie Latham, John Isaac,
Jason Semmens, and Mogg Morgan.

I've been cursed, I've been despised
As a witch with darkest powers
I shall go into a hare
I've been hunted, trapped and punished
In these my darkest hours
With sorrow and such mickle care

I've been thrown into the fire
But I do not fear it
I shall go into a hare
It purifies and resurrects
And I can bear it
With sorrow and such mickle care

I have outrun dogs and foxes
And I've dodged the tractor wheels
I shall go into a hare
I've survived your persecutions
And your ever changing fields
With sorrow and with mickle care

I will run and run forever
Where the wild fields are mine
I shall go into a hare
I'm a symbol of endurance
Running through the mists of time
With sorrow and such mickle care

*Source: Traditional Folk Song based on the Confession of Isobel Gowdie —
17th Century Witch. Adapted by Maddy Prior*

Published by
Mandrake of Oxford
PO Box 250
OXFORD
OX1 1AP (UK)

A CIP catalogue record for this book is available from the British Library and the US Library of Congress.

978-1-906958-23-7

CONTENTS

Preface to the Third Edition

Why the need for a third edition of my book after only five years
of publication? Too complex and troublesome to go into here,
but essentially due to circumstances beyond my control and as a
result of my own misguided altruism.

Things and life have moved on considerably since I first put
pen to paper as it were all those years ago. Most of what I wrote
still stands regarding the work I do; but no longer do I mix with
predominantly Pagan folk but a much more diverse community
that reaches worldwide now.

I have concentrated more on simply working with the Land
and my community. I wanted the images in this edition to reflect
this, so I decided to completely change all the photographs to
ones that are more up to date and show more of my work in
action.

So many books, (and I was guilty of this myself in the early
days) show purposely posed photos. Indeed in this day and age,
Photoshop has come into its own and has created some
wonderfully crafted images. The only drawback to this is when
folk believe those glamorous images to be reality and are fooled
and seduced by them. This happens when the boundary between
fact and fantasy becomes blurred—and some do this deliberately
for personal gain. I wanted to remain what I have always purported
to be, a down-to-earth, pragmatic village wisewoman. Hopefully
the photographic images in this book will record that fact.

A word about my contributors.

Angie Latham
Angie is an accomplished and successful artist and I am delighted
to be able to have her illustrations in my book that enhance the
text and chapters so well. I admire her hard work and diligence

to her professional commitments and I find her interpretations of the natural landscape truly inspiring and visionary. For more information on Angie and her work contact her website: www.celticmystery.co.uk

John Isaac
John first approached me a couple of years ago at the very first All Hallows Gathering at the Museum of Witchcraft & Magic, Boscastle, Cornwall. He wanted to work with me to build up a photographic portfolio concentrating on what he referred to as 'old style witchcraft'. His emphasis was on recording what was actually there, rather than finish up with a pristine, air-brushed version of the subject. This realistic, documentary style appealed to me and after viewing examples of his work, we agreed to collaborate together to produce the unique photographs you see in this book. None of them are posed and are taken whilst actively performing magical work. I think the authenticity of them shines through and I am well pleased with them all.

For more information on John and his work contact his website: www.johnisaac.com

I remain grateful to both Angie and John for their stunning contributions to this the Third Edition of *Village Witch*.

WALKING ON THE WILD SIDE

Wisewomen lead challenging lives. It has ever been thus, and in my opinion, will ever be so. It comes with the territory. I call it walking on the wild side. Let me attempt to explain...

Walking on the wild side is not a comfortable life. If you want security and a settled family life, forget this way, for it can drive you mad. It will take you to the edge and hang you over it - just because it can. It may produce sudden and unaccountable illnesses - illnesses that tear through the body in the form of strange fevers and violent purgings that will leave you grey and shaking. It will take you through very strange worlds, which you cannot find the way out of without surrender to the spirits. So, overall it's not a good career move for the faint hearted!

I have tried many times to live a relatively normal life, without much success. This lifestyle chooses you, stalks you and claims you as its own. It can be a solitary life at times. I am fortunate that I am surrounded by a very supportive tribe who recognise and acknowledge my role in the community. However, one to one relationships are another matter. It's very difficult to maintain an intimate relationship with someone who lives a medial life and is at the behest of the spirit world.

There appears to be a fashion at the moment of weekend workshops where you become a shaman or shamanka. This is not possible to attain over a weekend, and no amount of walking around with bits of dead animals hanging from you and going off into strange trances with accompanying odd noises will make you one. By contrast, anyone truly called to work with the spirit world will often have had a very chequered past where there are many instances of near death experiences, which are truly terrifying both physically, emotionally, mentally and spiritually. It has often been said that the line between madness and genius is very thin, and this is where the old magic lies. It is not found in DIY magic books - if there is any book, it is the book of nature, and nature is relentless.

In attempting to define the indefinable – this strange and fluid way of life – I can only use my own personal experiences as a village wisewoman to illustrate the way. No day is like another, no client is like another, every situation varies with the individual and my work continually evolves. This is not a path to personal fulfilment however; my greatest rewards are witnessing the fulfilment of other people through a process of deep healing that is triggered by the clients themselves. I am only a companion and helpmate to their journeys. The only surety is, that all things change, Love conquers all, and that Fortune favours the brave. It is a life of soul searching and soul rescue. Only when one has been through the dark night of the soul, or through the Underworld, can one be in a position to aid others through a similar process. Every time we enter the Underworld, something is left behind, a sacrifice for the gods. There have been many heart wrenching sacrifices in my life, but I wouldn't have it any other way for this is my true vocation this time around.

PROLOGUE

Let's set the scene...

The time is shortly after the first Lunar Eclipse of the 21st Century - a new Millennium. I am recovering from major surgery. Following this I had to face the possibility of a terminal illness, but thankfully got the all clear. So, facing mortality. Always a sobering thought - mortality... For me, the reaction was 'Eek! There's so much to pass on - I can't go yet!' - hence this book.

The place is sitting in a rocking chair by a roaring fire, in an old granite cottage on the outskirts of a small village, in deepest, darkest Cornwall. Musing about life, my life - where I've come from and where to go from here...

The reality is, I don't possess a rocking chair - just as well - I tend to trance out all too easily in them. I'm also not by the fire. I'm upstairs in my bedroom writing this where the temperature is bracing. I'm wearing several layers of clothing, including a body warmer and fingerless mitts, and I have a hot water bottle on my lap. I do have a heater but can rarely make use of it, as I can't afford to.

Of course some folk will always have very romantic notions around the sort of work I do. I am a village witch or wisewoman, registered with the Inland Revenue as a small business. How I got to earning my living in such a way is part of what this book is about, and there are many anecdotes to tell - some

13

good, some heart-warming, some hilarious, some scary, some tragic, and most soul searching.

When anyone asks me what my profession is, I usually get a strong reaction. Instantly their minds conjure up an image. Obviously it depends on where that person is coming from, as to what image is evoked.

The average person will firstly look incredulous and questioning – am I pulling their legs? Some then want to know more as it has captured their imagination. Somehow it has connected to what I call the primitive part of their brains. Like a race memory, they get in contact with the concept of the role I play within the community, and recognise its validity.

Others, being slightly unnerved, will ridicule and make jokes. I usually can get in there quickly with my own humour. I know most of the good witch jokes! F'rinstance:

"Ooo! Are you going to put a curse on me and turn me into a frog?"

I give them a long appraising look and say; "It looks like you don't need any help from me, my dear!" I smile sweetly and move on.

Obviously there are people out there who, because of their interpretation of their religion (usually a fundamental one), perceive me as a living embodiment of evil. This can be hurtful if you let it, but after all, it is an unreasoned response. Rarely do these people wish to discuss matters any further as they have already made their minds up, and are not about to look at the possibility of further information. The images of witch and scapegoat are inextricably and often unconsciously linked, as is the fear of possible contamination. Hence they end up being frightened by their own Shadow.

There do exist, thankfully, people who are fully and sincerely committed to their beliefs and see my

14

occupation for what it is – a vocation. They recognise that people are wonderfully diverse, and that being so, it makes sense that there are different religions to suit different people. They see through the various trappings and look to the heart and soul of the individual.

Then there are the folks who have a highly romanticised view of witchcraft and look back to some sort of golden age of magical arts, which in my opinion, never existed – except perhaps in their own minds. Unfortunately, at present witchcraft is "cool" and there are far too many questionable books surrounding the subject and currently swamping the market. And there is a market out there. People want a 'quick fix' to their problems, and what better way than to wave a magic wand to make all your problems go away? This, in my observation, is what happens with any unorthodox movement. Firstly it is persecuted, then it is ridiculed and finally, it is marketed. Certainly this has happened with witchcraft.

Image is very important, and to some people, essential! However, you often hear people say, "It's just my imagination." as if it decries the power of the imagination as something not worthy of consideration. One would find it very difficult to perform magic effectively without this powerful tool. The imagination is boundless. This can be inspiring for some, and very scary for others. Once again, it depends on your point of view.

In the Museum of Witchcraft at Boscastle is a section on Images of Witchcraft. There are a wide array of examples from various times and places. These illustrate how it is the image within the group mind of a particular society, which determines its attitude to witches. This can mean the difference between life and death.

Media has a powerful responsibility within society regarding what images are conjured up in the minds of the public. It has always been so, whether it be newspapers, TV, and film; or books, pamphlets and works of art. This is why I also work with the media to try and redress the balance regarding witches in society. Sadly we still have 'witch-hunts' nowadays, only it's not just witches anymore. It's anyone who is different in some way, whether that be their beliefs, colour, race, sexuality and so on. As a witch, I am very concerned with eradicating the witch-hunts. I'm not interested in battling, that just keeps the war machine fed. However, I am into disarming, building bridges and co-operation, so that we can meet in the middle ground and understand our differences. I believe that at the core of all religions and beliefs there is an essence of truth that is universal. The rest is just window dressing according to the personal taste of the individual. It's not any one faith that causes the world's ills – it's fanatics that do that, and they're found, sadly, within all belief systems.

Being a village wisewoman doesn't mean adhering to particular religious beliefs. It is rather the spiritual beliefs of the client that may well have a bearing on the work. Traditionally, village witchcraft utilised whatever was available at that time. That could have meant drawing from Christianity for various spells and magical chants. They were more likely to effect a positive response from the client to the work at hand. I tend to use whatever is effective for any given situation, irrespective of my personal beliefs. This is what is most important in magic – is it effective? Does it work?

Village Witch, hopefully, will go some way towards telling it how it is for a working village witch in the

21st Century, combining the physical reality with the magic of the Old Ways.

May you enjoy the journey, Reader...

EARLY DAZE

Never did I think for one moment that I would become a pioneer in anything, but I did when I became the first village wisewoman/witch to be registered with the Inland Revenue as a small business. As far as I know I remain the only person who supports herself entirely from her Craft. This unique position didn't happen overnight. It came about through all sorts of strange journeys and synchronicities...

Is one born a witch or do you become one? It's always difficult to answer that question, it could be either or both. All I can do is tell you of my own experience, which, looking back on things includes, both options. I certainly was not aware of witchcraft when I was a child, however I was using psychic skills without realising what I was doing, in order to survive.

It's not my plan to write an autobiography, time for my memoirs later maybe! However, it's not possible to talk of my life as a village witch without some reference to my past. After all, I am who I am because of the experiences I had...

I was born in the dead of night, on 6th March 1950. Life became very confusing and traumatic soon afterwards. After a few weeks with my natural mother, I was placed in an orphanage prior to being adopted. Weirdly enough, I found out much later that this adoption occurred on Halloween, a date which was to have particular significance in life...!

Almost immediately after I was taken from my mother, I fell ill with a fever (rheumatic/scarlet?), which left me with a condition that was quaintly called 'a susceptible heart'. Very apposite as it turned out!

My earliest memory is of lying in a metal cot, in a large room surrounded by crying babies, and I was screaming with rage. I was not picked up. In time my screaming stopped, and I remember trying to disappear into myself by curling up as small as possible, occasionally whimpering. This must have been when I was either in hospital or the orphanage. Some people find it difficult to believe that I have such strong memories of such an early age. All I can say is that although a lot of my childhood is blurred, my babyhood is remembered with extraordinary clarity. I can remember teething, what the rubber teat from a baby's bottle felt like, and nappy rash – yow!

Looking back as an adult, I don't find these reactions as a baby too surprising. After all, I was with my mother for about five weeks, time enough to 'bond', and then I was snatched from her arms and placed in a situation where I was not nurtured adequately.

Back in the fifties adoption was more of a hit and miss affair. Basically, if you could show that you were financially solvent and were an upright citizen, then you were granted adoption of a child. No consideration was given to psychological or physical compatibility. So there I was, placed within a family of strangers who were, as it turned out, totally incompatible to the sort of person I was. Talk about feeling like 'a stranger in a strange land'! I felt very alienated, alone and in the wrong tribe. I have a couple of photos of myself as a toddler and small child – it's striking how my expression is showing complete bewilderment.

Some say that adopted children need to consider

20

that they are special because they were chosen. Well, that may be so for a lot of people, but was sadly not the case for me – quite the opposite. Whenever I misbehaved, I was threatened with being sent back and a good little girl replacing me. I know now that wouldn't have been possible, but in the eyes of a child it was an all too real fear. One mother had already sent me away (so I thought) and here was another threatening the same.

The family I was adopted into was very strict and not given to displays of affection. Touch was kept to a minimum unless punishment was being administered, and then it became very physical indeed. Suffice to say that I cannot remember being sat on my parents' knees and being cuddled, but I do remember very well, being put over their knees and soundly spanked. I grew to live in fear of my mother's temper and disapproval, and started to try and avoid her attention falling upon me… and yet deep down I yearned for her attention – what a paradox for such a young mind!

I learnt how to become invisible – how to keep a low profile – how to camouflage and merge into the background…. but even this was not enough. So what I did was to escape into a fantasy world of my own, what I would call nowadays, the Otherworld. This world was wonderful, and was peopled with fairy folk and spirits of all kinds.

Back in those days, children were able to spend long hours out playing without adult supervision, and I certainly made the most of it. I lived (and have always done so) in the countryside, and spent many happy hours in the woods and fields around my home, talking and playing with the spirits of the trees, streams, stones and the like. I remember that, particularly in the woods, there were some very ancient characters, probably ancestral spirits, who I would often go and talk to about my problems. The trouble was, that I often lost track of time, which meant I was late home. I learnt very quickly that to tell the truth about why I was late didn't go down very well. However, it didn't seem right to lie, even if it meant avoiding a beating, so I learnt the skills of evasiveness and manipulation at a very young age.

Another thing that I used to do as soon as I was big enough, was to climb out of my bedroom window at night, especially when there was moonlight, and walk around in the countryside. Thankfully, these jaunts were never discovered as I had learnt how to hide in the shadows and not to leave traces of myself behind me. I was probably seen as a lonely child with an overactive imagination, but as far as I was concerned, I had lots of 'friends' and learnt all sorts of things from them...

My mother often called me a changeling, and once I knew what that meant, I incorporated that idea into my world and wondered when I was going to be released from my plight. I used to have fantasies about who my real parents were, and that once they knew where I was, then of course they would come and rescue me and claim me as their own. Of course, this never happened, but it didn't stop me from hoping that one day it might. It wasn't long before things took an even darker turn. There weren't organisations like Childline available, and certainly no one who I could go to within the family for help. It was a very confusing time. In fact, it wasn't until I was much older that I realised that what had happened to me as a child fell into the area of abuse. Violation often occurred at night when I wasn't fully conscious and it was hard to differentiate from dreams to begin with. Anyway, I think you get the picture.

As a result of these covert experiences, I developed

the ability to leave my body and to distance myself from what was happening – a handy survival tool given the circumstances. So, I had acquired the skills of shape shifting, invisibility and astral travelling at a very young age, and was able to contact the spirit world with ease – all without a witch in sight!

In trying to write descriptions of all the pertinent facts concerning my childhood, I'm finding that the whole experience is too overwhelming, too sad and too tragic. It's not until you start peeling off the layers of your past, that you realise exactly how painful it all is when presented as a whole. Whilst living through the experiences, you just deal with them as and when they come up. So, for now, I will present certain landmark situations, which have a direct bearing on what I was to become later on. It would need another book to relate all the gory details...

Puberty was certainly a landmark for me in that all these strange things were starting to happen to my body, and thus the energy directed towards me from other family members changed too. Sex, or anything remotely connected with it, was never, ever discussed – so you might as well have shrieked it aloud from the rooftops, the reaction was that intense.

I well remember being in the local haberdashers with my mother who was buying some buttons, and I had to whisper to her asking whether she could buy me a bra. She blushed deeply with embarrassment and bought the first one that was offered by the assistant. I felt dreadful, as my schoolmates had been taking the mickey out of me because I was developing rapidly and noticeably, and also it was getting painful without proper support. Why my mother didn't notice I don't know – well, I do now, but at the time I was genuinely puzzled.

Needless to say, when I first started menstruating it was

a complete shock to me – we didn't have sex education in those days – and I thought I'd injured myself in some way. Once again, having told my mother, the relevant accoutrements were shoved at me and I was left to get on with it.

Round about this time was when I first started to receive unwelcome attentions from another member within the family. I was informed that if I told on him, that no one would believe me – and he was absolutely right. No place to hide, except in my imagination...

So, I threw all my energies into performing well at school. I thought that if I was good enough, then my mother would love me, and the predations would end. I had just changed from the junior school into the local secondary modern and placed in the top class. I made a concerted effort to get good exam marks and it paid off – I came second in my class. I was jubilant, as I knew that was no mean feat in that particular class. I ran all the way home excitedly to show my mother my school report. I burst in the door yelling, "I've come second! I've come second!". My mother turned to me from the sink and coldly said, "Why weren't you first?". I was devastated. From that point I completely gave up. I knew that whatever I did would not be good enough for my mother, and that she set impossible standards that I hadn't a hope of achieving. Sadly at that time I didn't have sufficient belief in myself to succeed for my own sake. So the schoolwork suffered – I became the joker and larked about in all the lessons – I became a misfit, a disruptive element and was sent to a child psychologist. All the psychologist said was, that I had a higher than average IQ and that there didn't seem to be any reason why I could not achieve, ergo, it was my own obstructive behaviour that was at fault. Very helpful!

When it became time to sit my final exams my

parents decided that they were going to separate and asked me who I wanted to go and live with. I found it impossible to choose. If I went with my father I would be free of the adverse attentions of my mother, but I knew instinctively that my father was incapable of caring for me practically speaking. This was confirmed later on in life when he completely crumbled after my mother's death. If however, I went with my mother, although she could look after me I wasn't sure I would be able to deal with her anger. As it turned out, they decided not to separate after all, but this was after I had failed all my exams and left school with no qualifications whatsoever. Tragic really, as I had the ability and intelligence and it was wasted.

I decided to follow nursing as a career. I managed to pass the entrance exams and was accepted as a student nurse. My mother's response to this was "I don't know why you're bothering. You'll never amount to anything!" Well, I was bothering for all sorts of reasons. I desperately needed to leave home – I had run away from home many times as a child only to be brought back by the police. And I wanted to feel needed and vocational work fulfilled this for me.

I found this very satisfying at first and it worked well, but it wasn't long before I had problems with my personal relationships. When someone has been abused in any way, it leaves damaged instincts and these can cause havoc. To a certain extent I was still living in my fairytale world. I wanted a knight in shining armour to sweep me off my feet into the sunset, where we would live happily ever after. Well, that's not a very realistic point of view on life is it? However, it was an image that was reinforced by society at that time. You met a young man, you got engaged, and then you got married and had babies. Meanwhile, the sixties phenomena of 'the permissive society' was unfolding too, which made things even more confusing – for women. If you saved yourself sexually for marriage, you were square and old fashioned, but woe betide you if you succumbed before marriage because then you were a slut. Damned if you did and damned if you didn't!

Shortly after I started my training, I met a young man who fitted the category of eligibility required, and I dutifully 'fell in love'. Not with him, I now realise, but more with the accepted image on offer from society. We got engaged (on Halloween!), and married exactly a year later (on Halloween...). I knew the night before my wedding that I was doing the wrong thing, but didn't have the bottle to pull out of it. I should have known better, the record at number one in the hit parade on my wedding day was, 'Band of Gold' by Freda Payne!!

My new husband underwent an overnight transformation from an attentive, considerate boyfriend into a mean, and ultimately, malicious control freak. He worked in the police force, which caused many problems for me. It can be a very lonely and isolated life being a policeman's wife. I didn't fit in with all the other police wives, (Tupperware and gossip didn't appeal to me) and people just didn't trust you elsewhere. Many's the time that I know that conversations have been abandoned or diverted purely because they thought that I might 'grass' on them to my husband! It didn't help either in those days to build police houses in the middle of council estates – doesn't do a lot for neighbourly rapport. I wish I'd had the wherewithal to stand up for myself in the early days, but I found it too difficult and subsequently became a doormat. I had entered victimhood with gusto!

Things went from bad to worse with criticism coming not only from my husband, but also from 'the powers that be' within the police force. I was taken to task about what I wore and about my behaviour.... I never did fit in, wherever I went I seemed to be this quiet rebel, and here it was happening again. I retreated into illness and developed all sorts of complaints, probably most of them being psychosomatic, but they felt very real to me. I didn't know where to turn.

I knew I had to get away, but in those days you had to remain in the marriage for at least three years before any sort of divorce would be considered. So I persevered, and eventually, on our third wedding anniversary (Halloween), I packed my things and left home. I filed for divorce on grounds of unreasonable behaviour. My mother was deeply shocked by all this, and couldn't believe that I was giving up a lovely home, and bringing disrepute upon the family with something as distasteful as divorce.

My husband decided to turn round and grant a divorce on grounds of his adultery, which threw me completely. When I saw that the co-respondent's name was my best friend, I was stunned – I had no idea. Whilst I was still in shock, my husband moved quickly and commandeered all the marriage goods, and I was left with nothing - and too upset to pursue the matter further.

Needless to say I went into a very sharp decline after these betrayals, and attempted to take my life – I'd had enough. I'd bottomed out and couldn't see any ray of hope. Eventually I was hospitalised for depression and subjected to the exquisite torture of electro-convulsive therapy. This form of treatment uses the same technique as banging the telly when it won't work properly! I must have signed a consent form, although I really can't remember much from those days. Besides, the main side effect of ECT is short-term memory loss – this still happens to me nowadays and it can be very frustrating, although I have now learnt to laugh about it more.

I found humour to be an invaluable tool in my healing process. I have a very wicked sense of humour; a sort of gallows humour aimed at life in all its vagaries. Part of who I am and what I do is strongly connected to something called the Wounded Healer. These people have been initiated into this type of healing through the process of tragedy of some description. The wound never totally heals, but the very fact that the person has survived the past and is actively engaging with life in order to thrive, points to a healing of the Self by helping heal others in similar positions. Only the person who has already been through the mill can truly empathise with another. Otherwise you can only imagine what it's like – and for some that simply is not enough. They will only trust those who have been on a similar journey and returned – for the fear is that they will not return.

This description of Wounded Healer really resonated for me when I came across it. Much later on in life I began to understand more of the shape my life took, and why. Certainly I had a flash of connection when I read the following in a book called 'Mysteries of the Dark Moon' by Demetra George. She is talking about Persephone's Children...

"When daughters have the experience that it is their mothers who have left them alone and unprotected, they have a different kind of dark journey to travel than if they were the ones who were doing the leaving. The daughter may also lose her mother to death, to an alcohol or drug addiction, or to a debilitating illness. A child may be given up for adoption or into the care of another person, or taken away because of divorce. A daughter may feel her mother withdrawing from her emotionally and psychologically if she is neglected and beaten, or with the arrival of a new stepfather. And the most emotionally wrenching betrayal a daughter can experience is when her mother does not protect her from physical or sexual abuse by other members of the family.

What happens to Persephone children (male or female) growing up when they lose their mother prematurely in a devastating act of physical or psychological separation, and their mother is not there to take care of them? The descent into the darkness at such an early age can leave lifelong scars. The trauma of being abandoned into the underworld predisposes children to feel totally unequipped to cope as they are growing up with what they see as the confusion, uncertainty, and insecurity of life. This accounts for much of the depression, isolation, and lack of self-love and esteem that people carry when Persephone is an active archetype in their life. And yet, on the archetypal level, it is this very descent that opens a person to the wealth of the inner world and the secrets of renewal." (Page 254)

And

"It is not always an easy path for a person to have Persephone as a private muse. While she promises the wealth of the inner life, the road to her treasures is often an initiation by tragedy. Persephone encounters her rite of passage into the underworld

29

while she is still a young child. This goddess often arrives early in the life of her initiates, sometimes in violent and devastating ways, jolting them out of their childlike innocence. She may come cloaked in the garment of the death or dysfunction of a parent, the break up of a family, sexual abuse, or a major illness or accident that leaves a prolonged disability. The immature child is suddenly faced with a heart-wrenchingly painful situation that is beyond his or her emotional capacity to deal with.

For a sensitive child with a fragile ego, the trauma that accompanies feeling abandoned or losing a safe and secure environment leaves a lasting impression. The outer world is seen as a threatening place, full of uncertainty and terror, and the child feels forced to retreat into the inner world. The child learns to find a safe haven by withdrawing into the self, and begins to call "home" the huge emotional void left by the loss of love and security. Tragedy forces the Persephone child into the make-believe world of the inner life, but this event also leads to an encounter with the psychic forces of the unconscious.

Reclusive and highly secretive, Persephone's Children develop an aura of mystery around themselves as they grow up. They often need much time to be alone; it is in their isolation that they reconnect to the womb of their childhood nurturance. Projecting an ephemeral quality, as if they were somewhere else, they find solace and meaning in a realm that is not recognised or validated by society. Thus they feel alienated, uncertain of themselves, and yearn for invisibility.

They are driven to continually re-enter the darkness of their private world. If they have been fortunate enough to discover the hidden wealth of the unconscious, they can benefit from contacting this deep reservoir of unseen power. Accessing the intuition, detecting the movements of the psyche, understanding the meaning of dreams, communicating with spirits in other dimensional realms, dialoguing with the voices of the shadow, pursuing knowledge of the past and of the esoteric mysteries, and practicing a spiritual meditation are some of the gifts that Persephone offers to her initiates.

By a plunge into the underworld realm through an act of fate, the person guided by Persephone is gradually led to finding a vocation in the psychic arts, in alternative healing, in working with death and the dying, and helping those who have suffered much tragedy in their lives. As psychotherapists and counsellors they are skilled in facilitating a person's movement through life/death crises and psychological transformations and rebirths." (Page 258)

I know that was a long quote, but it was so apposite that I had to include it all. You can see why it had such an impact on me – it gave a recognisable shape to my life – and it made sense of it too, which is why I have included it here. I'm sure that other 'Persephone Children' will recognise themselves and hopefully be helped.

To get back to the story thus far...well, the scavengers and predators were circling... When you are wounded and vulnerable, certain types of people perceive you as 'prey', and home in. This is part of the victim/persecutor scenario. It would be a while until I realised how to break this particular pattern, but then I just fell for the next bait - hook, line and sinker! Very appropriate considering that I am a Pisces!

So I went through a process of having relationships with totally inappropriate people - people who were angry and violently passionate, who were into control and power games, who had hidden agendas and so on. At first these types of relationships can appear to work very well, and they feel very exciting. There is a strong attraction because each person is responding to their opposite. For instance, we may be attracted to someone who appears to be self assured, confident and dominant purely because we lack those traits ourselves, or, certainly in my case, want to be taken care of. Now the trick is to learn these qualities from the partner, rather than depend on them completely for it. Otherwise, if the partner is no longer there for any reason, we fall over because we have used them as a crutch. It brings up all sorts of issues regarding co-dependency whereas, in my opinion, a healthy relationship is about two individuals who choose to be together, rather than not being able to live without each other. Once again society encourages co-dependency - you only have to listen to a lot of love songs to realise this. "Without You" and "God Only Knows" to name just two - there are many, many more...I call it 'High Dependency' music!

Victim/persecutor set-ups call for collusion by both parties. They don't work in isolation, but it would be a while until I realised my input into my own pain. Meanwhile, I had many more epic misadventures to experience!

Now anger was an emotion that was not allowed expression in my upbringing - well, not my anger anyway! I had to obey without question - or else! So my anger was repressed. The trouble with emotional repression is that although it is fiercely controlled, because it's not familiar or known about, it can suddenly express itself explosively and without warning. It's a bit like sitting on a balloon - it's bound to pop up somewhere unexpected. What happened with me was exactly this. One day, through something quite minor, I snapped and my anger exploded with such a force that I completely and utterly trashed my room. The damage I managed to inflict with my bare hands went far beyond my usual physical capacity. I'm actually small and petite, but my energy was monstrous. As a direct result of this I was sectioned under the Mental Health Act and involuntarily hospitalised. The one time I had openly expressed my anger, and I was locked up for it! I had chosen the wrong time, the wrong place, and the wrong people.

You don't realise, until it happens to you, exactly how appalling being locked up feels. We don't appreciate our freedom until it is forcibly taken away from us. It's a very panicky feeling - "Will I ever get out of here? - Will the other 'inmates' harm me? - I want fresh air, I can't breath!" I'm purposely not going to go into too many details about what happened whilst I was incarcerated. I've already exorcised a few ghosts by a play being written about my experiences in a locked ward - it's called "What the Cat Dragged In." and I've got the theatre performance on video - very cathartic! Suffice to say, I eventually managed to extricate myself from that hell-hole and I set off on a search for meaning to life...it was as sure as hell not making much sense to me so far! I decided to actively search for spiritual truth and so began exploring different faiths.

Christianity seemed the obvious first choice due to the easy accessibility of it in this country. Also at that time, whilst I was back working on the hospital wards, I had been approached and befriended by someone who turned out to be a Born Again Christian. I found out later that this is often how people can be drawn into this religion in adult life. At a time of crisis, people are often approached by such folks, and encouraged to come to their church where there is a very warm welcome. This was very attractive to me at the time. I was lonely, vulnerable and unhappy, and anyone offering comfort and a sense of 'family' would have been irresistible – and was.

I started to attend her church and got to know her family. Then, due to unforeseen and dramatic circumstances, I was made homeless and I moved in temporarily with them. I became very involved with a group of people within the church who had started house meetings that centred on the teachings of the early apostles. This meant that there was emphasis placed on the gifts of the Holy Spirit – i.e. prophecy, healing, miracles etc. I threw myself 100% into the whole belief system and I found that I was a 'natural' when it came to some of these gifts - there were many instances of me successfully prophesying and healing people. I continued like this for a while, and during this time moved again to the household where all these meetings were taking place.

Now, to be totally honest, I cannot fully remember what exactly turned this energy from being productive and positive, into something more sinister – the people concerned would no doubt say that was my entire fault. All I know is that I was suddenly accused of being possessed by the Devil!

If you have ever watched the play "Oranges Are Not The Only Fruit" by Jeanette Winterton, you will have some idea what happened to me next...! When this play was first broadcast on television, it had a very traumatising effect on me, because it threw me back to

34

the nightmarish time that I am about to describe.

I was subjected to various methods of exorcising demons. They did it in shifts. I was forcibly held down and deprived of food, drink and sleep, whilst they ranted at me. This continued over three days apparently, by which time I was hallucinating and there were strange phenomena occurring around me – objects moving, light bulbs exploding and the like. They all fled, and I slowly regained consciousness to find myself in a wrecked room, with a policeman standing over me. After trying to explain to the police what had happened, it wasn't too surprising to find the doctor and social worker appearing yet again. Despite my implored appeals to them, I was taken away once more to the mental institution. Once in there, a deputation arrived from the church. They brought all my worldly possessions with them, after having gone through them looking for signs of 'witchcraft' (ironic now!). They told me that I was banished from any contact with their church and that it would be preferable if I left the area. So much for Christianity!

So there I was, back in the hell-hole... I didn't know it then, but fate was about to deal me the cruellest blow of all. I managed to find time to myself amidst all the chaos around me to consider things. I have a vivid memory of sitting on a windowsill by my bed at night (about the only peaceful time there). The moon had risen in it's fullness and it's light was touching everything with a magical glow. I thought about what I had been through in the last few months, and decided that although I was in accord with the gospel of Love that Jesus taught, I was having real problems with all the structures and strictures that surrounded his teachings. As I gazed at the moon I realised that I could no longer pursue this belief, and it was pertinent to me that the main icon of Christianity was an instrument of torture. I was imprisoned, but no one came to visit me, I had been made an outcast. This didn't fit in with my idea of love and compassion, and so I consciously cut myself adrift from Christianity, or what I now call Churchianity, and knew that I had to look elsewhere for my spirituality.

In the meantime I had to plot my escape from this place. It's really difficult to remain calm, surrounded by so many genuinely disturbed people, but I persevered only to find that I was accused of manipulation by the staff. Every week they had this assessment panel to see whether to continue the section orders or not. It felt exactly how I imagined the Inquisition would have been – they held your life and future in their hands. Eventually I was told that I would be released if I had a place to go to on the outside. I immediately phoned my parents who had retired and moved to Cornwall. I asked whether I could move down to be with them so that I could be released from hospital. I needed a fresh start somewhere completely different, with hopefully leaving all the bad memories behind. My mother agreed and everything was set up for me to travel to Cornwall.

It was the night before my release and my bed was surrounded with all my packed worldly goods. I was trying to get to sleep, which was difficult because I was thinking about my new beginning tomorrow. A nurse came into my room and told me to come to the office as the Charge Nurse needed to speak to me. As I heard these words I felt a sense of impending doom... I sat down in the office and the Charge Nurse said, "There's no easy way to say this. Your mother has just phoned through and cancelled tomorrow's arrangements. They have changed their minds about you staying with them. In fact, they don't want any further contact with you." So, my parents had disowned me. All the so-called friends I had were no more – I was completely and utterly alone in this godforsaken place. I had reached the Pit.

For a lot of people who have experienced any form of self-growth, I have noticed that there is a defining point where they turn their lives around. This moment had come for me. I literally had no one in the world I could turn to, and therefore, no one to utilise as a crutch. I had a stark choice between giving up completely, and pulling myself up by my bootstraps. Believe me, giving up was tempting – I was worn out, devastated and deeply wounded. It could have been easy for me to let myself slip into madness...at that time I would have been 'looked after' within the institution and probably have formed a 'career' of mental instability. The harder thing to do was to start from scratch and to become self reliant and self-sufficient. Fortunately I rose to the challenge. You can be certain that I would not be writing this book today if I had chosen the other option. Given the present political climate regarding the treatment of the mentally ill, I probably would now be homeless and destitute, wandering the streets, lost in a rambling inner world.

It's all very well making life decisions, but you have to back them up with action. My first priority was getting out of the hospital and into the world again. Not easy. I wasn't going to be released until I had somewhere to go to, and I wouldn't have anywhere to go to without a job. So, to begin with I looked for a job with accommodation thrown in. I realised very swiftly that I wasn't going to get the response I wanted with the mental hospital as a return address. Also I had references to consider, and given my past problems, they weren't going to be glowing. I was hunting for a nursing job because that was all I had been trained for, however it was pointless pursuing the usual vacancies in the

Nursing Times because of the above reasons.

I was determined to move forward, and so I persevered by getting permission to have day releases in order to look for work. The hospital was quite close to a seaside resort, so one day I travelled there and had a look around. On impulse I made enquiries at a holiday camp only to find that not only did they offer accommodation, but no direct references were required – just proof of registration. I'd found my way out!

Within days I had been discharged and had moved into the holiday camp and started work as a nurse at the First Aid Post. If I thought that I was in for a less stressful time, I was mistaken. I was expecting cuts, grazes and coughs and colds – what I got was, one attempted murder, one suicide, several muggings, and countless strokes and heart attacks! If we were called out at night we had to have a security guard with us for protection...and so on. Living within the confines of all this unpredictable energy, was very wearing. The accommodation left a lot to be desired, and the morning reveille of "Wakey! Wakey! Campers!" out of the tannoy was driving me crazy! Within a week I had found a small bedsit and moved in.

I managed to stay in the job for the season and then went on the dole. I really wasn't sure which direction my life would take from here, but at least I now had a good reference from my last job. There were quite a few people from the camp that were 'wintering' until the next season, and I spent quite a bit of time with them, usually in a pub. I suppose I became a bit of a waster for a while, but felt entitled to a bit of a break. I'd even plucked up the courage to write to my mother telling her that I was out of hospital, had been employed, and was endeavouring to make a fresh start.

For a few weeks we exchanged correspondence and this is when I found out that, much to my surprise, it was my father who had put his foot down about my moving to Cornwall. Due to my decision to turn my life around, I was writing to my mother in a very honest and straightforward manner. I was aware that maybe, just maybe, the ice was beginning to melt a bit between us.

One morning during that winter, I was awoken by a policeman hammering on my door. Why do we instantly feel guilty when the police arrive unexpectedly on our doorstep? My first thought was, what had I done wrong? After all, I'd got a bit squiffy on drink the night before... No. It was to inform me that my mother had died from a heart attack.

I was stunned. I didn't cry – I couldn't. I went round to a friend's house and told her. She called me 'a cold cow' because I wasn't crying. I didn't visit her again! I still was numb. I phoned my brother. He told me that my mother had been in hospital for a fortnight. Nobody told me this. He gave me details of when he was travelling to Cornwall and where I was to meet him. When we got there my father was not in a good enough state to deal with matters, so my brother and I took over all the arrangements. I wanted to see my mother's body and this was arranged by the hospital. I went on my own and was left alone with her for a while.

I entered a large grey, windowless room. In the middle was a trolley or table with a body on it. I walked over to it and gazed down at what was left of my mother. She looked dreadful. Being a nurse I knew that she had not been laid out with any sensitivity. She didn't have her teeth in, yet her nose was packed with cotton wool. Her hair wasn't even brushed. I felt angry on her behalf at her loss of dignity, and offended on my behalf. I couldn't experience any sense of farewell or closure with my mother looking like this, so I left the room. I wanted to take the matter further, but my brother totally refused and insisted that there were more important things to be attending to. Why did I want to see my mother dead, anyway...was I going 'weird' again? So, it was left – unfinished...and I still hadn't cried.

Things had begun to take on a rather surreal aspect, which was reinforced by my first time experience of visiting a crematorium. The first sight of it brought up feelings of unease, in spite of being set within beautiful grounds. Many images of the Holocaust came to mind and were added to by an air of 'business as usual' about the place.

Inside was a very functional and neutral looking room with a lectern at the front. The coffin was placed on, what I thought was, an altar to one side. The place was grey, unwelcoming and soulless. The vicar bore an unfortunate resemblance to a vulture. He was very tall and cadaverous looking, stooped, with a huge beak of a nose. He was dressed in a black robe and spoke in sepulchral tones. The air was dense with lugubrious energy.

After the committal was said, the coffin slowly rolled away through a small pair of curtains. I found this very disturbing, because the last thing I expected a coffin to do was to start to move under its own volition. And then to disappear (to who knows where – what's the other side of the curtain?) through rather theatrical looking curtains... I was left feeling like I was at some sort of bizarre and sinister music hall, especially as there was some very wobbly organ music being played at the time.

Our time was up so we had to leave. There was

another funeral party waiting as we left. We were guided to where the flowers had been arranged on an open space of concrete. I noticed that there were quite a few hearses waiting, and it all felt like a factory where the conveyor belt was chugging relentlessly on...and I was reminded of the Death Camps again. I was glad when we left.

Once home again in my bedsit, it wasn't long before I started to get phone calls from my brother regarding my father. The neighbours had been phoning because they were concerned about him. It became apparent that something had to be done, but my father refused all offers of visits. It was decided that I would move down to Cornwall to live with my father without telling him I was on my way.

It's a very strange feeling to be moving with all your possessions to a completely different part of the country, knowing that your arrival is probably going to be met with dismay, or possible aggression.

My father was rather ineffectual, and usually took the line of least resistance in order to keep the peace. He didn't do anger, so not too surprisingly, every now and then he really blew his top – inevitable when strong emotions are repressed over a long period of time. Believe me, when my father lost his temper, it was truly alarming. He once went berserk in my bedroom with a carving knife when I answered him back as a teenager. He also suffered from very dark depressions occasionally, when he wouldn't talk to anyone except to growl at them. These periodic outbursts were entirely unpredictable - at least my mother's tyranny was consistent!

So it was not an easy train journey and it seemed to take forever... Once I had arrived I needed to take the taxi man into my confidence, and explain the likely position I would be in at the other end. The plan was that I would knock on the door and go inside once my father had opened it. The taxi man would then unload my luggage and put it in the hall whilst I dealt with my father.

We arrived in driving, thrashing rain with the wind howling like a banshee. I braced myself, and then knocked on the door. My father appeared looking wild eyed and dishevelled. I launched myself at him and gently but firmly took him with me to the kitchen. I tried to divert him by talking about needing a cup of tea after such a long journey. He wasn't having it as he noticed what the taxi man was doing and tried to stop him. I managed to talk my way out of any violent confrontation, and the taxi man left me with my luggage and a very paranoid father. Eventually I got to bed in the early hours of the morning, aware that my father was pacing and muttering to himself outside the bedroom door. So, this was my new beginning...

The next few months were very difficult and demanding. My father showed all the signs of paranoia (with a persecution complex thrown in for good measure) – hearing voices, people on the television talking directly to him, me poisoning his food (he was convinced that I was plotting revenge on him), even the cows in the field passing coded messages! I went to consult his doctor but every time someone in authority came to visit and assess the situation, my father underwent a transformation and appeared logical and sane. Once these people were out of the door he reverted to his former delusions. Imagine how frustrating this was? It was my word against his, and given my history, no prizes for guessing whom they believed! However, things soon came to a head...

I was lying in bed one morning when I heard the sound

of a siren coming close. Retired people mostly occupied the estate where we lived, so I imagined that it was an ambulance I was hearing. Then I realised that whatever it was had pulled up immediately outside, as I could see flashing blue lights through the curtains. Before I knew it there was a loud banging on the front door, which my father opened and the hall was suddenly full of burly firemen! I threw a dressing gown on and asked the fire chief what was going on. He told me that they had received a call saying that there was a bomb in the house! Meanwhile my father was ranting saying that the oil heater was going to explode any minute. I quickly explained to the fire officer the position regarding my father's health and he understood immediately. The firemen took the oil heater into the garden and dowsed it with water, which seemed to satisfy my father. All this was very traumatic, but at least now I had some solid evidence of my father's illness and could get help for him – or so I thought.

An appointment was made for me with the psychiatric consultant where I explained everything to him. He said that if I could persuade my father to be admitted voluntarily, then they would treat him. Otherwise there was nothing they could do, as he didn't present as being a danger to himself or others. Well, I wasn't going to wait until that happened, so I endeavoured to persuade my father to come with me to the hospital to see the consultant.

To this day I don't know how I managed this, but I got my father on the bus. Once on board, he really started going to pieces, screaming and ranting that the bus was going to blow up! What a nightmare journey... When we eventually arrived outside the hospital, there was building work going on. My father took one look at the scaffolding and started to run away saying that he was going to be hanged for his sins! I grabbed a passing hospital porter and ordered him to fetch a member of staff from the psychiatric ward immediately. Within minutes, thankfully, a team arrived and took over, persuading my father to go with them. At last I could relax and let someone else care for him, and hopefully ease and treat his distress.

My father was kept as an in-patient for a about a year after that. I visited regularly, although I was asked not to in the early stages, as my presence seemed to agitate him too much. Once discharged, my father seemed a lot better and much calmer in his approach to life. I had found employment in the local hospital and had moved out into the nursing home. We met for lunch once a week and, in a similar way to my mother, began to make some headway with our father/daughter relationship.

At one of these meetings my father mentioned that he had to go to the hospital for blood tests. I asked what these were for, and when he said that they were further tests for anaemia, I felt alarm bells ringing. I made sure that I went with my father for these tests and that I was wearing my nurses' uniform. I managed to collar the doctor and asked him to put me in the picture. My worst fears were realised. My father had an acute form of leukaemia. Within a month he died, with me at his bedside holding his hand.

Still no tears. Another visit to the crematorium with all its bizarreness.

Now, I wouldn't be too surprised if you were thinking, what has all this got to do with witchcraft? Well, stay with me – I'm slowly getting there. All these landmark experiences make sense of what was to come later. Certainly as a result of my experiences with mental illness, death and dying and its associated rituals, I was determined to find a better approach to life than I had found thus far. I was convinced that there had to be meaning in this entire relentless trauma. My spiritual quest had been put on hold during this time, because there was so much going on. It's hard to explore any spirituality without any leisure time – one needs time for contemplation – which I wasn't getting.

So there I was, orphaned in my twenties, with no real sense of family or belonging. It doesn't matter at what age you lose your parents, and irrespective of the quality of the relationship with them, when they go there is a bereft feeling ...no bolt hole – not that I had one anyway, but you follow my drift?

Life carried on. I was made redundant from my hospital job due to cutbacks so I applied, and was accepted for, a job as nurse/companion to a remarkable old lady who lived in the wilds of West Penwith. Many people will recognise her – she was Rowena Cade, the creator of the Minack Theatre in Porthcurno. For those of you who have never heard of this wonderful place and person, let me give you a bit of a background.

Rowena Cade's family originated in Derbyshire and had an interesting ancestry as regards the Arts. One of Rowena's forebears (great great grandfather) was the famous painter of the Industrial Revolution, Joseph Wright who had a close friendship with Josiah Wedgwood – or so she told me. Both innovators of their time, and Rowena was certainly one herself within her time, 1893 – 1983.

The Minack Theatre is a unique cliffside open-air theatre, which has a most dramatic backdrop for the hundreds of diverse plays that have been performed there over the years. She created this extraordinary structure with the help of two local men only. No heavy equipment, but a lot of hard work and effort produced the fine theatre we have today. Rowena used

Porthcurno sand within the cement mix for the main structure, which consists of millions of discernable tiny shells, unlike the grains that you normally find on the beach. This had the effect of transforming the cement into a granite look-alike that merged magically into the Cliffside environment – so much so that many visitors are convinced that the Minack Theatre has literally been carved from the rock face and has been there since Roman times! Add to this the fact that all this sand was carried Sherpa style from the beach up to the cliff top by Rowena in the early days, and you get some idea of the strength of this remarkable woman's vision and determination.

My three years with Rowena were memorable. We developed a lively relationship, which was daily challenging. I did my best to maintain Rowena's independence, as she was now confined to a wheelchair, by taking her horse riding, visiting places of interest and bumpy walks along the cliff path. I also respected her need for privacy, when required, so we used to go through a little ritual every morning. I'd take in her wake-up cup of coffee and we'd have a short exchange about how she was feeling that day. I would give my input too and together we'd decide the day's events, irrespective of others' agendas and timetables.

Rowena was a very forthright person and certainly didn't tolerate fools gladly, but she also had a very ready wit. This was most apparent when she had visitors. People used to come from all over the world to see her, and occasionally there would be film crews who wanted to interview her. It was all I could do not to burst into giggles at Rowena's one-liner wry comments sometimes. Life was very stimulating at the Minack.

Although this wasn't the most lucrative post I have

held, it was more than made up for by the stunning landscape, which I lived in. My bedroom had a magnificent view, and I only had to sit up in bed to see Porthcurno Bay and the Logan Rock peninsula in all its different moods. Plus there was the theatre. I had free access to all performances and I made great use of this perk. I think that my experiences of this rekindled my interest in theatre and became one of my reasons for pursuing this later on at Dartington.

I eventually left Rowena and the Minack, as I had to have major back surgery. Sadly a few months later I heard that Rowena had suffered a stroke and was in hospital. I was told that there was no point visiting her because she was in a coma, but I knew better than that. The last sense to go in levels of consciousness is hearing, and it's the first to come back. This is why I remain very aware of what is said around unconscious patients. I sat by Rowena's bed, held her hand and chatted away to her for some time. Then I distinctly felt her squeeze my hand. Somehow I knew that was her goodbye to me. Sure enough she died a few hours later without regaining consciousness.

I made the decision not to attend her funeral, which I knew would be extremely crowded. I had already made plans to travel to Greenham Common for an Easter demonstration, and I knew that this action would be more in keeping with Rowena's ethos, as she couldn't abide any fuss. So, when that magical moment happened when thousands of people from all walks of life eventually joined hands around the U.S. Base at Greenham Common, I was honouring Rowena. It was a truly moving experience.

I have great respect for Rowena Cade and I feel privileged to have shared a small part of her amazing life. There's something about that generation that survived two world wars that produces some wonderfully eccentric characters who give something special to society. I often think of Rowena, and I miss her lively mind and vital presence; but her spirit lives on in her unique creation, the world famous Minack Theatre.

I first came into contact with St Buryan whilst I was living at the Minack with Rowena Cade. It sits on the main route to the Theatre and has mini rush hours every summer that you learn to avoid if you're wise. One day when I was driving through the village I noticed a small cottage that was For Sale. I had come into an unexpected inheritance that left me £17,000, and since I came from the generation that set great store in property as an investment, I was casting my eye around.

I made an appointment to view and was duly shown around by the owner. It was a traditional one-up, one-down, granite Cornish cottage. Inside it was like Steptoe's back yard! Every bit of space was taken up by umpteen TV sets and countless piles of old magazines, which was slightly odd as the owner was registered blind...

However, I looked beyond the crumbling plaster and peeling wallpaper and was enchanted by it. Most of the original features remained underneath, nothing was straight and the whole place was full of little nooks and crannies – just my style. So I put in an offer of £13,000, which was accepted, and The Dolls House was mine!

Thanks to my live-in job, I was able to do lots of work on the cottage in my spare time. Several friends helped with various bits including Rowena who rolled her sleeves up and built me a Minack grate. One of the first things we did was to reveal a glorious inglenook fireplace that you could walk into. I reckon it used to house a Cornish range as the fireplace was flush to the floor, and the massive chimney didn't have the right kick to it when we tried to light a fire. So Rowena built up a grate and inscribed the date on it. She was very particular and insisted on using the sand from Porthcurno beach for the cement mix. This sand is visibly made up of tiny seashells, and it's this combination that gives the granite-like effect to all the stonework at the Minack Theatre. Eventually I had to have a fireplace built within the inglenook, but it replicated the lintel shape so it looks like a portal within a portal. I use my hearth as a magical working space, or altar, and the whole set up is a very good aid to focus down on the work at hand. Interestingly the hearth is sited in the North East, which traditionally is considered to be the Portal in a magical circle.

Then we stripped the walls of what must have been at least ten layers of wallpaper and revealed the original granite walls. After repointing and waterproofing they looked great. The kitchen is very Heath-Robinson and is unusual in that the floor is much lower than the field that it backs on to. Also, there's a glorious view of Chapel Carn Brea (First & Last Hill in Cornwall) from the window, which I never tire of gazing at as I do the washing up in the mornings. This kitchen is actually part of next door's shed (or Annex as they like to call it). Sadly the deeds that cover the time when this was added to the cottage are missing (1878 – 1915), but I like to imagine that this transaction with next door happened over a pint in the local pub – there's certainly no written evidence to explain it. Talking of deeds, I have the original Indentures from 1825, which are amazing to handle and read, realising that the Prince Regent was on the throne when this peasant dwelling was first erected.

Acquiring my cottage was achieved through

spontaneity and intuition, and it wasn't until I started to live in the village permanently following Rowena Cade's death, that I fully realised what a truly fascinating place it was.

An interesting development occurred when I actually moved in. I was chatting to some old boys who were sitting in the sun at the market cross. They already knew that I had moved into my cottage, and asked my name. I told them and they started chuckling and suggested that I go and look at the house deeds. I was intrigued, and as it happened, I still had the deeds with me so poured over them that evening. The cottage is about 180 years old, so there was a lot to plough through, including the original indentures. Then I found what they were chuckling over. Back in 1937 the occupier was Cassandra Rowell. Well, I was amazed – I have rarely come across anyone with the same Christian name, but to find that on the deeds seemed like a good omen. They remembered her, and apparently she had eight children. Goodness knows where she put them all, as the cottage is called The Dolls House for a very good reason – it's tiny! Anyway, it felt like a good omen, and was – I still live there.

Fascinating as this is, I seemed to have deviated from the story of how I eventually found witchcraft – although I still maintain that it found me...

The next thing to happen in my life was that I was admitted to hospital for major surgery on my back. I had, over the years, developed scoliosis, which is curvature of the spine. The pain I was experiencing was escalating until the only option left was surgery. The operation consisted of inserting rods into my spine and I spent 6 weeks in hospital followed by nine months in plaster from my neck to my hips. During my convalescence I at last had some time to continue my spiritual search.

It was at this time that I started to explore Buddhism.

I went along to an open day with a large group of Buddhists and was introduced to chanting, which I thought was a method of trance work in order to achieve an altered state. I was assured that this wasn't the case – nevertheless I sat in a large room surrounded by dozens of people who were avidly chanting. Suddenly I was aware that a woman near the front was experiencing an epileptic fit. Nobody seemed to be taking any notice of her, so I made my way over to her and applied first aid. I pushed people away to make space for her. The chanting continued, and if anything increased in volume. Afterwards I asked why no one helped her, only to be told that the chanting would have helped her. Well, I was not impressed by this at all, and told them so. To me, any spiritual belief has to be backed up with practical application. That was the end of my foray into Buddhism!

Finally, at last, one Midsummer's Eve, I met a couple of witches.

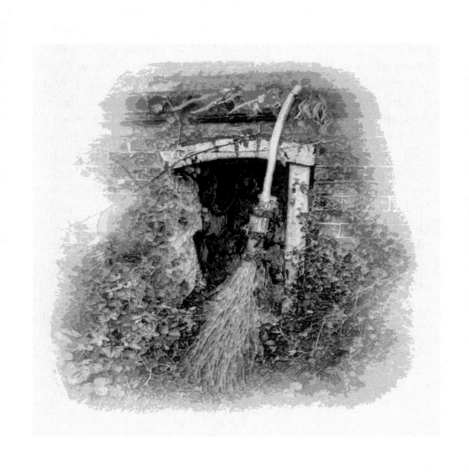

COMING OUT OF THE BROOM CLOSET

I have always had a curious, questing mind, and to be introduced to a couple of people who claimed to be witches, I found fascinating. I met them at a friend's house, and before I knew what was happening, I was asking them all sorts of questions. What was witchcraft? What did it entail? We talked for hours about the subject. I was introduced to such concepts as the Goddess, the Horned God, and the Wheel of the Year, the Otherworld, the Four Elements and Magic. These were all evocative terms for me. I was subject to the same conditioning as most people in this society, and a lot of these terms I had not come across before.

I did notice that I had an understandable knee jerk reaction at the mention of the Horned God. I tapped into the usual Denis Wheatley type image of the Devil with horns etc. I learnt that this image was simply a symbolic representation of the god of the wild and nature. Sometimes seen as Pan. This is where the word 'panic' originates from – fear of wild places. Certainly this panic can overcome people when they're out in the woods or wilderness. The half goat, half man represents our animal nature.

That made sense to me. We are, after all, part of the animal kingdom, however much we like to think of ourselves as being elevated above such things. I had always disliked it when anti-social behaviour was described as being beastly or acting 'like an animal'.

Animal behaviour can certainly be more civilised than a lot of humans' in my opinion!

I learnt that the image of the Devil was a scapegoat for our Shadow side, and that we often like to blame our dark side on something external to ourselves. Pagan belief was about personal responsibility - to live with and come to terms with our Shadow. I also learnt that dark does not necessarily mean evil - that darkness adds definition. If there were only light and no darkness, we would be blinded – in the same way that we would be equally blind with all darkness and no light. Therefore to incorporate both within our natures is more balanced and healthy. So, the Horned God simply represents the instinctive, and natural energies within us. Sadly, because of past fundamental religious indoctrination, the pagan idea of 'Old Horny' had been hijacked and presented as Satan, the Devil and God's adversary.

What I heard about the Goddess gladdened my heart. Through all of my explorations through various beliefs so far, the role of woman had been sadly maligned. At best, woman was perceived to be man's helpmate but still secondary to him, and at worst the ruination and downfall of mankind! As a woman, it was refreshing to come across a belief that placed the role of women in a more powerful, respectful way. Women were placed on an equal and complementary footing. I learnt about the strong connection between the Goddess and the moon – the moon and menstruation – and about the different phases and cycles and what they represented.

It all made so much sense to me. To perceive and understand the different seasons and the celebrations and festivals that marked the progress of the Wheel of the Year. I realised how disconnected society, and subsequently humanity, had become from the natural world. No wonder as a society we had become so stressed! In our arrogance we had placed ourselves above such things and had attempted to exert control over nature. This attitude is compounded by God's command in the Bible to Adam, to subdue the earth and to have dominion over it. Well, we only have to look at the forces of nature in action to realise how puny we are in comparison. Much better to reconnect and work with these energies rather than against them!

What I was told about the Otherworld took me back to my childhood. It reconnected me to the world I escaped to - only now I could enter it with impunity and wonder, and it was like meeting old friends again after a long separation. I could now enter this parallel universe with ease and utilise it. It was wonderful to discover that my way of perceiving the world around me was not 'mad' but inspiring. I had always seen every thing as being sentient, as having spirit, and here was a belief system actively encouraging this behaviour - what a relief!

We all talked avidly for hours and continued the conversation whilst I walked home with them along the seafront. As I was told about the different festivals, I realised that it was Midsummer's Eve and that I was impinging on their celebration, and told them so. No problem apparently as it was all part of the magic of that night. We eventually parted and I walked home (all of six miles) in the dawn half-light. I felt so inspired and had a strong feeling of connection and of coming home. At last I had found something that seemed to suit me down to the ground. It all made such sense and I was eager to know more. I'll never forget that walk home through the fields. I was looking at life and nature in a completely different way - it was beautiful in all its forms and I felt elated. Maybe this was what I had been looking for all my life - time would tell.

My life took on a very intense quality. I was well motivated by what I had heard thus far about Paganism. I wasn't totally committed to the witchcraft side at that time - too many old fears and prejudices to overcome. So we concentrated on learning more about the pagan slant on life, and had decided to set up a little rite of dedication to what were called the 'Old Ones'. (This is a term that I still use nowadays to refer to my sense of divinity.)

I was taught the pertinence of creating sacred space. This was nothing to do with being, or acting, pious. This was something very pragmatic and down-to-earth. Working with the elements of earth, air, fire and water helped with this process. It was primarily about creating, with deliberation, a space where I felt safe and secure enough to be myself in my true form. This was in essence a place of power, and meant subsequently, empowerment for me. This was the 'place between the worlds' where the magic happened. Magic was about changing things – changing matter – changing form – changing patterns. Powerful stuff!

Almost immediately I realised its potential, its power and tapped into it. My teachers, (because that's what they were at that time) said I was a 'natural'. Certainly I found working with these elementary magical principles simple. Notice I didn't say easy! It seemed to require a simplicity of mind that was quite childlike in its operation. You know the kind of thing, just like the child in 'The Emperor's New Clothes'. To believe in what you are seeing, because what you are seeing is your truth, despite other mixed messages that may be around. I have since called this way of looking at the world, and particularly the worlds magical, the Fisher Price approach. To encourage that simple, childlike wonder – to know that magic works, not to just hope it does.

I often have to remind myself of the early days of my witchhood. I can allow life to get too complicated sometimes, and once I realise this, I go 'back to basics'. Now I am aware that this statement caused an awful lot of problems to a certain Prime Minister not so long ago...but I suppose it depends on what your idea of basics are, as to whether that is a productive experience or not! I have a lot of affection for my early steps into witchcraft – a bit like the affection we feel when we watch toddlers making their explorations of discovery into the world. But that's just what it was like – I was entering a new world, full of wonder and wander! The magic fascinated me – I was like a kid with a new toy.

Not everything turned out the way I'd planned. Mistakes? I made a few, but then again, too many to mention! However, this is how you learn. Intent is all. So long as the intent was honourable, I felt the gods were patient with me. I learnt by my mistakes, but because I had such a healthy respect for the powers, I learnt how to deal with magic safely very quickly – thankfully. There's no room for arrogance when you're dealing with such energies. I was taught ways of 'setting up my circuits' so to speak, so that the power could be directed and utilised with effectiveness. I was learning a craft, and I was becoming totally absorbed into the process. It was round about this time that I realised that I wanted to take the step further into witchcraft, rather than simply staying with living a pagan lifestyle. I told them of my decision, that I wanted initiation into witchcraft. Very soon afterwards plans were made for that crucial ritual.

There is a lot to be said for the pupil having to wait a minimum of a year and a day before being initiated. That way, you have a whole year's cycle to work with the different energies of the Land and the Self. The principle being, that there is an inner landscape as well as an outer. I was thrown in at the deep end by being initiated after only six weeks. As it turned out, I was able to withstand the huge impact of this, but I certainly wouldn't advise it for everyone. Maybe my past adventures helped me through this particular process. Anyway, being thrown in at the deep end you definitely find out whether you can swim or not. Weirdly enough, sink or swim has strong connections with witchcraft, as this was a form of torture for unfortunate souls accused of witchcraft in the Middle Ages. The accused, nearly always a woman, was trussed up in a ritualistic way and flung into the nearest body of water. The test was if she floated she was guilty; if she sank she was innocent. Bit of a no-win situation what! Fortunately I swam – strongly, and against the current of my past life. I was turning my life around, and I was fully aware of it happening. I sensed on a soul level that becoming a witch would change my life irrevocably – I was right.

Before I knew it, the day had come that we had decided upon for my initiation. We had chosen the nearest Full Moon to a festival called Lammas or Lughnasadh. This year it had fallen on August 11th. A day of some importance I was to find out much later on – but that's another anecdote for later in the book.

It so happened that we were taking part in a local feast day on that crucial date, so I was in a carnival atmosphere from the start. I have photographs of me on that day, dressed as a gypsy and looking radiant!

I have noticed over the years that it is very difficult physically to get to a Rite of Passage, and this was no exception... I didn't have a car in those days, so we were left to find our own way back to my village – we had missed the last bus. We tried thumbing a lift, to no avail. We ended up walking the full six miles home in fancy dress (probably why we didn't get a lift – one of us was dressed as a Devil!). Then we got ready for the trek across the fields to Boscawen-un, an ancient stone circle.

I remember it being a warm summer night, lit wondrously by the Full Moon. We fought our way through the undergrowth, which was considerable. Eventually, after a lot of misadventures we arrived at the circle. I was left at the edge whilst they unpacked the different tools they had brought with them. When I spotted a sword I must admit I wondered to myself, what was I doing out in the middle of nowhere with a couple of people I had only known for six weeks – and they had sharp objects with them! I could see the headlines – "Local woman found dead from stab wounds in Black Magic ritual"! I managed to quell my fears and willingly entered into my Initiation Rite.

Now I'm not going to go into detail about this. Everyone's initiation is personal to him or her, and as such is private information. Anyway, I don't want to spoil it for any future initiates! Suffice to say it was the most powerful and magical experience of my life, and certain things happened that left me in no doubt of the authenticity of the ritual.

Afterwards I felt a definite shift in energy and perspective. I had performed the rite successfully, I had passed the test – I was a witch! Wow! It's difficult to explain how I felt, but it did feel like I had come home. I had joined a kind of sisterhood, an ancestry – a tribe. I felt for the first time in my life that I belonged and that felt great! Almost immediately the energy shifted and I was in contact with the darker expression of that. I smelt wood smoke, I felt the heat of the flames and I heard the screams of my predecessors being tortured and slaughtered. It was an extraordinarily powerful experience that I have never forgotten.

So there I was, a fledgling witch with the paint not yet dry on my 'L' plates! I was raring to go...I had a hunger and thirst for more knowledge and I avidly applied myself to research and gathering information about witchcraft. I scoured bookshops and libraries and found that there wasn't a huge amount of material. It definitely needed to be hunted down – unlike nowadays where there is a plethora of occult titles. I was an eager pupil and learnt quickly. It was strange to find that everything I was taught sounded familiar, and I realised it was more a case of remembering the Old Ways rather than it being new information. I was sent on quests and given exercises and tests that were very challenging, to say the least. I'll give an example.

One night I was sent out to gather 13 ivy leaves from a grave and to then return without looking behind me. Sounds easy enough, but believe me when it came to doing it, it was another matter. The moon was up and shed a ghostly light over the cemetery. I realised what a taboo I was facing. If I were caught there'd be hell to pay! However, I decided that wasn't exactly productive thinking and reminded myself that I wasn't out to do harm.

I shinned over the wall and made for the nearest grave, hoping to collect the leaves and be out as soon as possible. That was when the penny dropped, and I realised that ivy wasn't on the neat and tidy newer graves – they would be on the older ones in the most gothic looking part of the cemetery – and a long, long way away from the exit point. That got my hair standing up on the back of my neck, I can tell you! Often, graveyards are situated on old pagan sites, and as such are considered sacred to the ancestors. I was very respectful of the spirits I could feel all around me as I hunted amongst 18th Century graves. I eventually found what I needed and scuttled back clutching my ivy leaves. On my return I was instructed to make a protection charm with them. I succeeded in doing this and the charm was very effective due to the potency of the ivy leaves. The fact that they had been gathered with such highly charged energy made the whole charm buzz with magic. That's when I learnt that you get out of magic what you put into it.

As fascinating as learning the basic skills of witchcraft was, I also had to apply my mind to how I was going to earn a living. Considering the impact of major back surgery that I'd undergone 18 months previously, it looked like my former profession of nursing was out, at least for the foreseeable future. The DSS sent me on an Employment Rehabilitation Scheme based at Plympton, Devon. It was a six-week residential course where you had the opportunity of trying out different skills with a view to re-training. Whilst there we had to sit various intelligence tests to get an idea of what we were capable of. At the end of the course a careers officer interviewed us.

I was recommended for computer work and was put forward for a residential training course specifically set up for disabled people in Dartington, Devon. I was also asked what I would really like to do given the choice. I answered that I had always loved drama (no surprise there given my life so far!), and that I would like to train as a drama therapist. This is where I first heard about the possibility of doing a Degree in Theatre based, strangely enough, in Dartington, Devon. At first I baulked at the thought of attempting a Degree, but the officer assured me that the intelligence tests I had done showed that it was well within my capacity to do this. That was good to hear, so initially I applied for both. The computer course interview came first which I passed with flying colours. This gave me so much confidence that my interview at Dartington College of Arts was also successful. I knew which one I wanted and went for the Degree in Theatre, and committed myself for the next four years to some very demanding work. It's amazing how many people regarded a Degree in Theatre as a doddle – they had visions of people playing games all day! Well, it was tough work, because unlike the Art and Music students also there, we had to use ourselves as material. Often we would work 13-hour days, not only working on our own stuff, but also working in other students' pieces as well. It was truly exhausting, but well worth the effort.

It was a sharp learning curve but, fortunately for me, I discovered very quickly that there is a close association between theatre and ritual. This made it possible for me to continue learning about witchcraft as well as performance skills. Contact with my witch friends in Cornwall had fallen away and so in essence I was on my own. I had been initiated into a further level of the Craft before I left home so that I could operate independently.

Financially things weren't so hot, because although I was receiving a grant, it didn't stretch enough to keep my cottage running as well as paying rent in Devon. A kind benefactor, who lent me money to cover my costs with my house as collateral, sorted this problem – in effect I took out a private mortgage. It was a risk I was prepared to take in order to obtain my Degree.

Dartington is, or certainly was, a very alternative sort of place and I found that I could be open about my beliefs, which was very encouraging to me. It was quite something to be in an ambience that accepted witches! About halfway through the course I decided to start up a coven and performed a beacon ritual to call to me like-minded people. This was very effective and within a moon had gathered to me four people – three guys and one female. This coven subsequently continued unabated, with a few changes in membership, for the next 10 years. No mean feat!

After four very exciting and challenging years I gained an Honours Degree in Theatre. That was an edifying moment and I recall going out into the grounds of the college after I read the results. I stood beneath the trees and called up in my mind all the negative statements my adoptive mother had made about me not amounting to anything. I felt jubilant that I had proved her wrong and was now an Honours Graduate.

So what now? I hadn't a clue what to do next. All I knew was that I wanted to go home back to my village in Cornwall – so I did just that. The theatre course had helped with my physical recovery and I was reasonably fit as a result. As a consequence, since I had a mortgage to pay off, I re-entered nursing. The next few years I spent diligently working at a local nursing home on night duty.

The work was hard and the pay was peanuts, but then that was what it was like down in my neck of the woods. At that time Cornwall had the lowest wages in the country, at least nowadays there is a minimum wage in operation. Nevertheless, there is a lot of rural poverty where I live and for centuries the Cornish have had to eke a living where they can. Having said that, there is also a good sense of community because practically everyone is in the same boat, so you help each other out. There is a thriving Letts Scheme locally and a lot of skill exchanges happen as a result. It's more a case of coming together through adversity and diversity. You certainly have to utilise ingenuity to survive, but that's a good life skill, in my opinion. I had learnt that life didn't fall into your lap, vacuum packed. Thank goodness, I say – I never could fight my way through those wrappers very easily!

Little did I know it, but life was soon going to be irrevocably changed for me yet again...

On top of my work at the nursing home I was doing some agency work, which involved travelling to clients' houses for insurance medicals. I had just left a client and was travelling home for my tea, as I was on duty that night. It was a beautiful spring day and I was admiring the hedgerows as I drove along the country lanes. As I approached a double bend, suddenly, out of nowhere, a car appeared from around the corner. It was obviously speeding because the car ended up right on my side of the road. There was no way I could avoid a head on collision.... and that's all I remember until I came round to an ambulance man leaning over me. The transit van I was driving at the time was a complete write off. I realised I was lucky to be alive. Earlier in the day I had to decide whether to take my own saloon car or use the work van. I'm glad I chose the van - otherwise I would not be here now!

I was rushed to hospital and treated for shock and spinal concussion. After several weeks off sick I returned to work, but found that due to my injuries I was no longer able to work adequately. I persevered for a while although it was painful and exhausting, but in the end had to give in to the fact that the accident had effectively halted my career in nursing. My doctor confirmed this in writing and I became unemployed. The next four years were some of the toughest to endure. I wasn't getting enough money to pay my mortgage, and because it was a private one the DSS were not obliged to help in any way towards it. My

1. Walking the Land near Boscawen un stone circle with St Buryan in the distance. Photo credit: John Isaac

2. Conjuring the spirits. Photo credit: John Isaac

3. The Author at her cottage door with partner, Laetitia.
Photo credit: John Isaac

9. Mab – the Author's dearly departed familiar.
Photo credit: Apex Photo Agency

4. St Buryan churchyard gate.
Photo credit: John Isaac

5. The village of St Buryan from nearby stile.
Photo credit: John Isaac

6. The entrance to St Buryan Church. Photo credit: John Isaac

7. Reading the Tarot cards. Photo credit: John Isaac

8. The Author visiting the grave of the colourful local wisewoman, Granny Boswell (1813 – 1906), bringing 'Spingo' Granny's favourite tipple as an offering.
Photo credit: John Isaac

10. Clutterbuck – Laetitia's cat. Photo credit: John Isaac

11. Working cord and knot magic. Photo credit: John Isaac

12. Raising the energy. Photo credit: John Isaac

home was in jeopardy. During this time I learnt how to live on very little including 'gleaning' from the fields. Gleaning is picking up the remnants after a crop has been lifted. Somehow when I did this it felt timeless, and certainly the meals I made from my gleanings were delicious. Maybe I was getting in touch with the 'hunter/gatherer' in me! Also I was dealing with a long and protracted compensation claim against the young idiot that had ploughed into me.

I made myself useful by managing to get funding (from Dartington again!) so that I could undergo counselling training. After two years of hard slog and emotional rummaging, I emerged with my certificate of qualification. Another string to my bow – but I still didn't have a clue where to aim that bow!

The coven had continued in spite of there being a different base, but I was finding myself becoming quite dissatisfied with the set-up of me running the group. I tried to take a back seat and encourage others to take a more leading role, but that didn't work out the way I'd hoped. A group is only as strong as it's weakest member, and I was feeling that I was missing out on my own experience by making sure that everything was OK for everyone else in the coven. In the end I pulled out and resigned, and sadly the coven then folded. I had hoped that it would continue without me, but it wasn't to be.

However, it wasn't all gloom and doom – now I was left to my own devices magically speaking. Having left the formality of the coven, I could concentrate on what I wanted and be more spontaneous. I was aware that my approach to magic was becoming more primitive and down to earth. I roamed the countryside; I sat and listened to the Land and the spirits. By becoming solitary I had opened myself up to being taught directly by the Old Ones. I learnt, what is sometimes referred to as, 'cunning craft' from the energies and environment that surrounded me.

I don't know how, but obviously word got round the village and locals started to visit me asking for spells and charms and suchlike. They always came under cover of darkness, which was fine by me – I preferred keeping a low profile. I didn't charge money in those days, but I did receive quite a few gifts that were left anonymously in my porch. This was very satisfying and I felt that I was really becoming part of the community – and that felt rewarding on a soul level. Incidentally, this still happens nowadays where I will find a dozen eggs, or kindling and logs left as gifts. This generally picks up in the autumn and to find a sack of potatoes from a local farmer to see me through the winter is very much appreciated. It's a very warm hearted feeling and always makes my day.

I had a quiet uncomplicated life at that point – but all that was about to change irrevocably and this is how it happened...

After being unemployed for several years, I was eligible to attend the Job Club. This was a set-up where you could use lots of facilities in order to chase employment – computers, telephone, stationery etc. The Patients' Charter had just been introduced and one of the guidelines was that the spiritual needs of the patient should be addressed as well as the physical. This gave me an idea, which I acted upon by phoning the Senior Chaplain of the local hospital for an appointment. I told him that I was interested in putting my name forward as a Pagan Minister who could visit pagan patients. He granted an appointment the next week and I prepared for it by creating a CV. That was quite interesting – I was well qualified to do the job, but it did make unusual reading!

The interview was very successful and rewarding. The Chaplain had made up a booklet for the different faiths he was likely to come across on the wards, and asked me to check whether his entry for Pagans was correct. I left some booklets and further information with him about paganism and then departed with the knowledge that I was on the list of ministers, subsequently confirmed in writing. I really felt I had achieved something that day.

I had joined the Pagan Federation and was running the local Pagan Moot. A moot is an old word taken up by pagans to mean a gathering of like-minded people. It was great for networking and meeting new people who were interested in pagan ways. After my success with the hospital, I informed the moot that should anyone be unfortunate enough to end up in hospital, then I was available to officially visit them as their minister. Soon afterwards a friend from the moot approached me and said that her friend was a journalist on The Cornishman − a local weekly newspaper. He was very interested to hear of my appointment and could he do a short article for the Woman's Page? I thought about it and decided − why not? It would be for information purposes only, and it was only going to be published in a small weekly newspaper right down the far end of Cornwall − no one would take much notice of it apart from locals... How naïve can you get? My main concern was the locals in my village and their reaction. Everyone knew what I did, but it was never openly talked about − but I decided to take the risk, had the interview and waited for the paper to come out on the following Thursday. Without realising it, I had put certain things into operation that were to completely change my life around − talk about ignorance is bliss −

if only I'd realised!

Now I'm definitely not a morning person – never have been – never will be! Apparently I was like it as a child too – awake most of the night and sleepy during the day. Mind you, it was useful when it came to night duty... anyway, come that fateful Thursday morning, I was lying in bed thinking that the phone downstairs was ringing an awful lot...

I went downstairs and checked the ansaphone, which had about eight messages on it. The first was a journalist from the Daily Mail who wanted me to contact him. At first this puzzled me, but the phone ringing yet again distracted my thoughts. I picked up (something I don't do nowadays – I need to know who's on the other end!) and the call was from the Hospital Chaplain. He was very upset by the article that had come out in the paper. I hadn't had a chance to get the newspaper yet, so didn't have much idea of what had been written. He said that the hospital had been inundated with queries from the media about my 'appointment as a hospital chaplain'. I tried to reassure him that I had not represented myself in this way, and that I had no idea that the media would swoop to such an extent. After that knuckle rapping, I thought I'd better get the paper pronto and see what had been written about me. There it was, not the small item of information I was expecting, but a large picture of me under the heading of 'Priestess Cassandra is first Pagan chaplain in hospitals'. My heart sank. No wonder the chaplain was annoyed!

The phone didn't stop ringing all day. The story went nationwide and television companies approached me as well. The Big Breakfast and Richard & Judy wanted me to appear on their shows, as well as Westcountry News. I had to think on my feet very quickly. Obviously I was 'out of the broom closet' and realised that there was no going back, but neither did I want to become part of some kind of media circus. So I declined appearing on the chat shows, and decided to work only with the regional TV news. Even with that, it made the top story of the day – (I still have the video recording of that programme – I look like I'm in shock – I was!)

I had a funeral to attend later in the afternoon and I was wondering what on earth the reaction from the locals would be. There had been a spate of deaths in the village the previous week. I couldn't help thinking as I was sitting in the church pew, that a couple of hundred years ago it wouldn't have taken much for the villagers to turn around and point the finger of suspicion at the witch! To my relief, after the service I bumped into one of the stalwarts of the village who congratulated me on the newspaper article, and many locals backed this up.

I came home to a further thirty odd messages, all wanting something from me – apart from one. I'll always remember it. "Hello. My name is Sarah. I don't want anything from you. I just want to say, well done!" That single message was like a breath of fresh air in the midst of all that intensity. Eventually I met up with Sarah and we became (and still are) close friends.

Meanwhile the world continued to go mad around me. The next day was taken up with having a film crew in. This was an experience I hadn't had before and I was very nervous. I so wanted to get it right – whatever that was...I found myself worrying about the most inconsequential things. Now, as my friends no doubt will tell you, housework is not a top priority for me. Quentin Crisp was absolutely right when he said that after a couple of years, dust doesn't get any thicker! Besides, cobwebs go with the territory! Yet here I was getting concerned about what my place would look like on TV! Where was my head? For those who are

interested, dust does not generally show up on TV –
so it's as well to realise this if you find yourself in a
similar position – don't waste your energy polishing and
dusting, it doesn't matter!

I had no idea what I was going to be asked, but I
thought that they're only going to ask me things that I
know about already. Besides, earlier in the day I had a
very useful tip given me regarding the media; "Always
remember they want you more than you want them."
(Very true and has been invaluable ever since.) The
interview went well, and when I watched the TV
that evening, I saw that they had brought a vicar in to
comment. He looked totally bewildered and ended up
suggesting that pagans ought to be put in side wards!

It was during this time that I began to receive lots of
letters from people wanting help. At first, this disturbed
me as many of them were very needy, and I have a very
tender heart for such things. After all, I wouldn't have
been a very good nurse without having compassion. It
also had a rather wobbly effect on my confidence. I
had been working quietly on my own for so many years,
now I felt a bit like I was public property. My initial
reaction was to withdraw; besides I needed the space to
consider what had happened to my life. No chance of
that for a while!

For the next few weeks I continued to receive a
great deal of media attention, unfortunately much of
which tended towards sensationalism, and I certainly
didn't want that. So when I was asked to dress up, I
answered "Robe? What robe? When I work, it's usually
outside in comfortable clothes and wellies!" I had to
deal with the problem of the tabloids as well. I just told
them courteously that I was declining interviews for
their sort of coverage. I was told that the broadsheets
wouldn't touch such material, but that was fine by me.

(Incidentally the tabloids proved to be wrong in this assumption), I was more concerned that I was being represented appropriately, as this was an opportunity to set a few records straight regarding the general public's view of witchcraft. Although the pagan world doesn't have leaders, I knew that I would be perceived by some as being a kind of spokesperson, so I was determined to come from a point of integrity. All this was very wearing and eventually things eased down a bit, so that I could regroup. I used to have such a quiet life...but no more, which is why I protect my privacy as much as I can.

Over the next few months I was asked to give talks on Paganism at various small venues. My acting training stood me in good stead. I had found that I could naturally create a rapport with an audience, and given the subject matter, which was close to my heart, these talks were very successful. Then, that winter I was summoned by the Jobcentre to attend the dreaded Restart course.

For those of you who haven't had the dubious experience of this, let me explain. When you are in receipt of any government benefit (whoever's in power), you are obliged to jump through many potentially humiliating hoops – this was just one of them. Restart is a sort of Mickey Mouse type set up where everybody is treated only slightly above moron level, and taught to write letters, answer telephones, and how to conduct yourself at interviews. Attendance is mandatory, and morale was low.

However, this particular Restart course had obviously gone 'up market' and involved pop-psychology...and so we got the exercise involving Transferable Skills. We had to list what we perceived to be good transferable skills. Ever someone to make the best of a bad situation I put, and subsequently read out, "Excellent Tarot reader. Accomplished spell weaver, and maker of charms,

71

talismans, etc...." Once I had convinced the tutor that I wasn't pulling his leg, and I showed him the newspaper cuttings, he asked whether I had ever considered going self-employed as a witch.

Well, I'd often said that all I really wanted to do was my craft, but had spent my time searching for a niche out there in the world where I would get some sort of income from my skills. This is when I realised that there was no niche, and it was as simple as just get out there and do it. Back to my old saying, "If you can't find what you want, knit your own." Fortunately at this point, compensation was looming from the accident after four long years. So the outcome of all this was that I continued on benefit for a while – I was in their good books – because I was enrolled in the Business Start Up course.

This was fun! I recall the first day. We were all sat around a long table and we went round introducing ourselves and the nature of our business. You can imagine it...Hello! My name's George and I'm a Lorry Driver. - Hello! My name's Fiona and I'm a Potter. - Hi! My name's Cassandra and I'm a Village Witch!

Another amusing moment happened when we had a talk entitled 'Bad Debts'. I started grinning. I was asked what was so funny by the tutor, and then he realised what the joke was. "Oh, I get it. Nobody would want to be in debt to a witch!" Exactly so! Superstition is so useful sometimes! You don't have to do anything, except suggest – then leave it all to the imagination! Wicked!

I had been considering what to do with the money I received from compensation and now it was clear. I would pay off the mortgage, which would leave me with a small amount of money, which I decided to invest in myself. I registered with the Inland Revenue as a small business on the Spring Equinox 1997. I was interviewed on the local television news about this, and off I went into the world as an official village witch.

I found that I had all sorts of decisions to make. How would I present myself to the general public? What would I charge for my services? And so on... I found it helpful to view the whole situation pragmatically, so for the purposes of setting up a structure, I put all I do into a business framework and then adjusted things from there. There seem to be a lot of examples out there of creative people who never get their work off the ground because of poor business sense. Well, I'm no businesswoman, for a start I have dyscalculia (number blindness), but I do have close friends who are canny business people. They gave me a lot of solid advice regarding my venture, which has stood me in good stead and has kept the stress and pressure regarding the business side to a minimum. In fact, it was one of these valuable friends that first suggested writing this book. "Cassandra," he said, "You're like a folk singer without an album. You need to write a book – it will help lift your business." Wise words.

I found great difficulty when it came to deciding what to charge. My background was very sparse and bleak materially speaking as well as emotionally. I then went into a vocational profession, which is notoriously poorly paid – (why is that?) So the outcome of it was I had a sort of 'poverty mentality'. I was never used to a lot financially speaking so my expectations were low. Put this together with the fact that I live in a part of the country where there is a lot of rural poverty, and it's not surprising that I first set my rates ridiculously low.

Another thing that was happening in the early days was that I was trying to be all things to all people. Well, that's not humanly possible and I soon learnt to make the right adjustments so that my business and I would survive. I learnt to be intuitive with my clients so I was able to sift through and direct my energies appropriately. I raised my fees for one-to-one work to something more realistic, and I charged for consultation when approached by the media. That way the media work subsidised my income so that I could keep my rates low for my clients.

There were all sorts of issues going on for me regarding self worth as well. It's quite difficult for someone who has been wounded by their past to emerge with a natural feeling of competence and confidence in their work. I had to do some quite deep work on myself in order to connect with the value of my skills and that my labour was worthy of hire.

As a witch working in the 21st Century, and realising that presentation is important nowadays, I created a leaflet that explained what I did. I spent quite a long, considered time compiling this and included in it my Personal Code of Ethics. I felt that it was crucial to be clear about the parameters I worked within. There are not many – only three:

"Full confidentiality is assured.

Works of magic are only performed with the recipient's full knowledge and permission.

Any requests for work, which knowingly causes harm to others, will be declined."

Later on a website was created for me as a result of a skill exchange, with more information including a page about my cat familiar, Mab. Her story is full of unusual events too! I know that some purists within the pagan community shy away from technology, but I think to myself – work with the materials available. If the Internet was around in my predecessors' time, then I'm sure they would have utilised it. It's a big market place out there and I'm just setting up my stall...

This might be a good point to mention what it's like living on the edge, which is part of being a village wisewoman. The work is erratic, no question. It swings from feast to famine. If your security lies in having a steady income and lots of material possessions, then I would not recommend this lifestyle. If, however, you are willing to be able to turn your hand to most things magical; to live on your wits; to expect the unexpected; to really appreciate the gifts that life can give you if you let go of too much planning; to live for the moment and to rise to that challenge everyday of your life, then you will be good wisewoman material, in my opinion. One thing I can safely say about my work is, it's not boring!

A wisewoman's approach to her life and work could be summed up in the adage "Do the best you can with the material available." I set great store by this saying, and I would add to it that the practitioner is also used as material. I don't believe you can perform witchcraft effectively without being changed by it yourself. There is a strong emotional connection between the wisewoman and the work she does for others. This sort of work can exact a high price, but the prize is knowing yourself, as well as gaining knowledge from the other realms.

Certainly a large part of my witchcraft comes from a close connection with the spirit world. In order to establish and maintain contact with this shape-shifting world, there needs to be surrender to the spirits. Did you feel a slight shiver when you read that? Good. This is not a practice I would advise everyone to try – to enter into dialogue with spirits without due thought and consideration for the consequences. Now before anyone thinks "demonic possession" let me explain a little more.

I believe that everything has a spirit – even so called inanimate objects are sentient to me. I'm not that unusual. How many people do you know who have an ongoing relationship with their cars? Many give them personalities; they notice the connection between what's wrong with the car and what's going on in their lives; some even give them names. How many times have we all lost our temper with devices and gadgets? Not the best of relationships – but a relationship, nonetheless. Many people talk to their plants, and so on. Well, I've simply expanded and deepened that connection with everything. This also has a very powerful effect on the psyche and brings all sorts of things up to the surface. I believe this work demands commitment and I well remember the time when I made the ultimate commitment; when I offered myself in service to the spirit world. I said, "Whatever it takes!" Since then there have definitely been times when I have reconsidered that oath, but hand on heart, I have no regrets. It may be wild, and the spirits can roll you around and lead you up the garden path – but there are some wondrous things there. It makes life a lot simpler for me. I still make decisions in my life but there is also part of me that gives in gracefully to the spirits. (Well, mostly that is!)

You must have had one of those days when everything seems to hold you up – when you must be at a certain place at a certain time – and the day starts to fall apart? That used to really wind me up. Now if those sort of things start, I simply relax and wonder who I'm going to meet that I wasn't planning on, or what possibly negative event I have missed by being late. Far less stressful! Better late than dead on time...

There are also little dedications I do as a matter of course everyday. These help with maintaining the relationship with the Old Ones, as I refer to the spirits sometimes. So, I start every day by stepping outside, preferably with my feet on the earth, and I say Hi to the day – nothing elaborate. Once I'm washed and dressed I choose a Tarot card for the day. To me, this is allowing the gods access in order to give advice. So many times the daily card has been absolutely spot on! Every time I eat anything I bless the food and give thanks, a bit like a Christian says grace, and raise my glass in honour of the gods who have once again provided for me.

This makes me answerable to no one save my gods. If I'm destined to continue this work, then the gods will provide the wherewithal. In this way I get less entangled with the anxieties associated with the logistics of life. This leaves me free to concentrate on my craft. The gods will provide and I make sure I thank them.

It would be very remiss of me as a village wisewoman, not to tell you something about my village as the energies of it have directly informed my Craft.

I was aware from the start that St Buryan had very powerful energies and moods. Mostly observed from twilight onwards, the village sometimes has an intense brooding character to it. I liken it to a sleeping dragon, guarding its treasure. A bit fanciful maybe, but it best describes the quality of atmosphere.

We appear to have our very own weather system. Often you only have to drive outside of the parish boundary to find completely different conditions. Sometimes it feels like the fog descends from a pulley in the sky, it's that sudden and that thick! St Buryan sits on a high plateau of granite which seems to draw the sea mists and cloud down to ground level; and on the rare occasions that we have snow, it can cut the village off within an hour as all roads to it have substantial hills. Our storms are adolescent and come straight off the Atlantic Ocean, which surrounds us on three sides. It's easy to see the direction of the prevailing wind as the few trees we have all point in the same direction. The thorn trees in particular can be sculpted by the wind into the most extraordinary shapes. In fact, some do say that witches live in these trees...

I have found out some extraordinary facts regarding St Buryan's chequered history over the years. We are fortunate to have an excellent resource nearby in the Cornish Studies Library contained within the Cornwall Centre, Redruth. I was like a kid in a toy shop when I first discovered this wonderful place. Masses of information, access to old documents, maps, books and manuscripts, excellent copying facilities and staffed by a very efficient and friendly team of people. It was whilst I was happily burrowing away into this material that I realised what a debt of gratitude we owe to some. There were countless examples of travellers, usually gentlemen, visiting Cornwall and its antiquities and writing their findings. Thankfully they also spoke at length with the locals about the old tales and folklore of the region. They are delightful to read as often the language is old fashioned and quaint. For instance;

> "After a pleasant scramble through heath and gorse, we regained the carriages on the high road and proceeded direct to Land's End."

Thanks to the many books and papers written on the subject of the history of St Buryan, I have quite a few tales to tell. So let's start at the beginning...

St Buryan is a place of great antiquity with its first

traceable documentation in the early 10th Century. This is confirmed again as a settlement in the Domesday Book:

> "The canons of St. Buryan hold EGLOSBERRIE; it was free in the time of King Edward [before 1066]. 1 hide [120 acres]. Land for 8 ploughs [requiring, perhaps, 8 oxen each]; ½ plough there. 6 villagers and 6 smallholders. Pasture, 20 acres. Value 10s; when the Count [of Mortain] received the land, value 40s. Exon Domesday adds that there were "12 cattle; 12 sheep".

So what was there before this time? I have often wondered about this. There are many documented instances of ecclesiatical monuments erected on ancient pagan sites, and I have certainly felt this to be the case in St Buryan. So convinced of this was I that most works of magic I have performed have involved circumnavigating the precincts of the churchyard – fortunately there is a path that follows the entire church wall. It appears that St Buryan has been a place of power for many thousands of years, and recently I came across an archeological report which confirms this.

In 1985 the local Highways Dept decided to widen the main road through the village which necessitated taking out part of the churchyard wall. Cornwall Archeological Unit grabbed the chance to excavate that part of the churchyard, and they subsequently found the remains of a defensive Iron Age/Romano-British round. The report makes fascinating reading and can be found in the Cornish Studies Library in the periodical, Cornish Archeology No.26.

The appearance of Athelstan and the Charter he alledgedly granted to the village in the 10th Century was to cause huge repercussions over the centuries. King

Athelstan had come to Cornwall with an army in order to eject the last of the Danes. He spent the night before this final battle in the Oratory at St Buryan and decreed that if the morrow's battle was sucessful, then he would build a church for St Buryan. After the victory Athelstan duly granted land and endowments within said Charter. Later on this manuscript was used as evidence to procure what is known as a King's or Royal Peculiar. This means that the parish, which then included St Levan and Sennen, were exempt from jurisdiction of the diocese of the Bishop of Exeter. (Although St Buryan is no longer a Royal Peculiar, fragments of this remain in the fact that the church choir are still allowed to wear red.) Anyway, this Charter didn't sit well with the Church and all sorts of conflicts ensued over the years ending up in 1328 with the Bishop of Exeter (Grandisson) issuing no less than three sentences of denunciation and excommunication against the inhabitants of Buryan and placed the whole parish under an interdict.

Apparently when an excommunication was called for it was usually uttered from the nearest church dedicated to St Michael. This was because St Michael was seen as the 'dragon slayer' i.e. the archangel who dealt directly with fighting pagan ways, or dragon/earth energies. In this particular case the nearest place to perform this awesome ritual was St Michaels Mount in Penzance where the Great Interdict was performed by 'bell, book and candle'. This means that a candle was lit which represented all the souls within Buryan, the Interdict was read out or rather "the thunder of the Sentence against the people of Buryan":

> "As these lights are in bodily manner put out before our eyes, so in the presence of God and of the blessed Mary and of the blessed Angels and of all

Saints, may their souls be put out and handed to the devil and his angels for punishment without end in everlasting fire, unless they repent and come to their senses: May it be so; may it be so!" (translation from Latin)

The book was then slammed shut, the candle upended and extinguished, and the bell tolled. Heavy stuff indeed, but then there are over 200 curses in the Bible. Ironic when you think that illwishing is usually laid at the door of witches. This particular excommunication was not lifted until eight years later.

In 1351, writing to the Bishop of Worcester, Grandisson states that he is afraid to meddle with St Buryan for no one belonging to him dares go there for fear of death and mutilation and:

"who below the Apostolic See can absolve them for their enormous crimes and excesses? I am silent concerning mere rumour, but it is lawful to speak of what is manifest to all. Since these men are in the tail of the world, they are constituted almost like wild beasts, they contract marriages in every prohibited degree and are divorced in every lawful one."

Even nowadays many look askance when St Buryan is mentioned, and no wonder given its anarchic history.

Another gift of Athelstan to St Buryan was the establishment of a Chartered Sanctuary. Ordinary sanctuary granted immunity to a thief or debtor provided they remained within the precincts of any church for up to nine days. However, a Chartered Sanctuary extended to lifetime immunity so long as the miscreant kept the King's Peace within the boundary which was usually one to two miles from the church. In St Buryan's case the area covered one hide, or 768 acres, and many believe that the large circle of stone crosses which circumnavigate the parish are markers for the Chartered Sanctuary.

What is intriguing is, that there are five roads which all meet around St Buryan Churchyard, and then there is the large circle of stone crosses 2 miles away – with a little stretch of imagination you can discern a pentacle in the land!

According to local knowledge there have always been witches in Buryan. This is great because I have the priviledge of keeping an old tradition alive, thereby becoming part of country ways. This is supported by local folklore collected by such luminaries as Bottrell, Hunt and Quiller-Couch where there are many tales of wisewomen/witches and their escapades.

There are darker tales too which could explain why the village was used as a setting in the cult movie 'Straw Dogs'. I know that quite a few of the villagers were upset by the film when it was first released because they felt that it was an adverse portrayal of the village. However, it wasn't a film about St Buryan and its inhabitants – it was a dramatic fiction, but I bet that Sam Peckinpah was picking up on Buryan's ancient potencies. Its history is anarchic and even nowadays it attracts eccentrics and is consequently very diverse. I think that secretly the locals quite enjoy the notoriety...

I remember a few years ago an incident which illustrates this point. It was winter, and I had walked to the pub admiring the Christmas lights that had been erected. I was particularly taken with how lots of the lighting tableaux represented the different occupations of some of the inhabitants. For instance, outside the home of a fisherman were dolphins, a lighthouse for an ex-Navy man and so on. A few hours later I returned home to find an astonishing spectacle outside my cottage. Emerging from the bushes was a Witch on a broomstick in purple neon lights! Once I'd recovered from the shock, I approached my friend who was responsible for this creation. His response to my concerns over whether this would sit well with the locals was: "The St Buryan Lights Committee wanted to show and celebrate the diversity of the village." Fantastic! I do smile everytime I see it illuminated each winter.

I enjoy a simple life within my community, and hold many villagers in great respect as they have had to work extremely hard and shown great courage through many tragedies and upheavals. I admire the sturdiness of the Cornish spirit, especially the 'Dreckly' principle. For those who haven't come across this before, it's summed up in the following allegorical tale:

Spanish fisherman in conversation with Cornish fisherman:

Spanish fisherman: "Is 'dreckly' the same as 'man yana'?

Cornish fisherman: "'ell, no – not that quick!"

So much of modern life, particularly 'up country', is lived at breakneck pace. It's great to live in a place that finds time to smell the roses so to speak.

Since I believe that 'home is where the heart is', I will probably spend the rest of my days living in this unique village, where I am quietly proud to hold the title Wisewoman of Buryan.

WORKS LIKE A CHARM

One of the questions I get asked more than anything else is, "How do I become a wisewoman?" Well, in my opinion, it involves quite a few ordinary, but important things. Observation tops the list. If you're going to work in the community, you need to know that community.

In the old days when there was less opportunity for travel, the village wisewoman would know a fair amount about everyone in her village. In fact, she probably would have been there at the births and deaths, as this was a role often taken by such folk. Much of the village wisewoman's work sprang from observing her community closely, thereby acquiring in depth knowledge of what was going on. In the eyes of less observant people, this could appear magical. Her work spread by reputation and word of mouth - for good or ill - thus was she imbued, by her community, with 'special powers'.

You need an enquiring and questing mind. Get in touch with that 'Fisher-Price' side of you. What happens when you do this, as opposed to that? What's the outcome? Is it effective, does it work? (Interestingly, scientists and inventors will often work this way invariably with serendipitous results.)

Also watch the tides – and I don't just mean bodies of water. A study of correspondences is needed. What phase is the moon in? Is it waxing or waning? What astrological sign is it in? At what time does the planetary tide shift from one energy to another during each hour of every day?

Obviously you can't carry all that information in your head, but at the very least, you need to know where you can look it up. After all, if you were a fisherman you would consult not only the tide tables, but would observe the weather, moon phases, and seasons as well. All this information is very useful in order to link in with the appropriate energies. This enables you to choose the most auspicious time to perform specific acts of magic.

There are many books available nowadays containing correspondences, usually as appendices. Correspondences are lists of different objects and concepts which have particular qualities or virtues associated with them. Books on symbolism are also useful, and an ephemeris (tables of planetary movements) is needed to know what influences are happening in the heavens. It's as well to remember that, apart from the ephemeris, these books are written from the author's point of view, as indeed is this book. Therefore, it is better to find out, by trial and observation, what works for you.

There are many in the Pagan world who insist on maintaining certain traditions and for whom 'tradition' itself is all-important. Tradition, as far as I'm concerned, represents something that a body of people have found to be effective. This does not mean that tradition therefore has to become dogma. I went so far as to look up 'tradition' in the dictionary and found that there was an emphasis on tradition being passed down from person to person and usually orally, as opposed to being written down. The problem with writing things down is that you run the risk of it becoming some sort of Holy Writ where nothing can be altered. This is where fundamentalism can creep in where people attach far more importance to the letter of the law rather than the spirit of it. In my opinion, tradition needs to be living, vibrant and ever evolving. You may, through experimentation, find that some approaches work differently for you. This is what you work with – that which works for you no matter what others may say. All anyone can do is offer guidelines. Listen to your own resonance.

So, we've looked at observation, an enquiring mind, and I will add another important factor – pragmatism. It's so important to keep your feet on the ground, especially if you are dealing with the spirit world and all things magical. I'm sure we have all heard many tales, or maybe have met people, who are not grounded and have ended up as 'space cadets'! If you are going to journey through magical realms, it is imperative that you are able to find your way back again to the physical. Believe me, some ill advised souls do get lost and sadly never find their way back to reality.

In my work I listen to many stories and I make sure that I reality check everything. So much of the Old Ways involve psychology after all. More of which later.

It's no good having wonderful magical concepts if they are never going to be manifested. Spells and magic need to have a practical application if they are ever going to be effective. Sure, the mind is a powerful tool, and as such needs expression in matter – otherwise, it will simply remain in the mind as a concept only. Magic needs action to move it on. Also, by being pragmatic, it stops you from getting above yourself. It's not wise to mock the gods – they can have a wicked sense of humour! The Greeks called this sort of arrogance, 'hubris'.... and they have a powerful Goddess figure that presides over it – she's called Nemesis – I'm sure you've heard of her!

All too often the village witch is viewed as some all

powerful, magical being – which she is not. Anyone has the ability to tap psychic energies and perform magic. It's a question of whether people choose to develop these skills or not. Therefore, the witch is no better or worse than any other professional individual. You get egotistical prats in all walks of life, but we seem to have more than our fair share of them nowadays within the witchcraft movement – don't let's add to them! I assume that there is an evolutionary purpose for having prats on the planet, but I have yet to work out what it is.

Many churchmen warn of the dangers of dabbling in the occult – and I have to say that I wholeheartedly agree. Dabbling is extremely dangerous in certain pursuits. Magic can be perceived as akin to electricity. The power source is neutral. It depends on how you set your circuits up as to whether the power will kill or cure. Picking up a screwdriver does not make an electrician. So, I do not advise dabbling. Get to know your subject and then approach with care and respect before experimenting.

Whilst using the electrical metaphor, I will extend it by confronting the issue of 'good/bad' magic. If you wish to create a charge you have to bring positive and negative together. It's no good trying to work effective magic by ignoring your dark or Shadow energy. You need to bring all of your witch power to the fore, not just half of it. All-positive energy will not produce that magical spark any more than all-negative will.

I personally feel that any witch worth their salt needs to have the ability to curse as well as to heal. When I mentioned this on the 'Kilroy' programme a few years back, it caused a tremendous furore. I was more or less accused of being evil for even thinking about cursing. (i.e. I must have done evil deeds in order to have the ability.) What I would have said, given the opportunity, is if I had a black belt in karate, I would have the ability to kill with my bare hands – however, I wouldn't need to kill someone in order to get my black belt! But more about cursing later....

The main difference I have with the Church is that it teaches that dark power comes from an evil source, whereas I believe that it is the operator of the power source that will decree a good or bad outcome.

So, on to another concept that is often misunderstood... Chaos. This is a word that has taken on rather negative connotations in our society. It's viewed with suspicion and yet all it means is:

> "Formless void, great deep of primordial matter, abyss from which cosmos was evolved." – Oxford Dictionary.

Chaos is very important and pertinent in the scheme of things. Whenever there is death of something, whether that is a living thing, a relationship, a habit or anything that comes to an end; then there always follows a time of limbo or chaos, until rebirth. Let me put that into a simple metaphor. Take the caterpillar, which eventually turns into a butterfly. The caterpillar spins its cocoon, and rather than, as I used to think, change one suit of clothes for another, it breaks down into a sort of soup from which the butterfly eventually forms. There is a liquefaction stage where there is no form – this is chaos.

When we see plants dying back in the winter months, rebirth doesn't spring up immediately. Everything looks dead, but deep within the soil lays the seed that is crammed full of potential. Only when spring arrives do we see the new form appearing above the surface. In the same way, part of one's inner growth process requires a period of limbo or chaos. Especially when you are working with deep-seated patterns, it is important to remember that an old pattern cannot be turned around overnight. When we stop negative habits, it's not immediately apparent what to do instead. What's the new form going to be? Well, it requires patience and application – it will become apparent with time. It's never easy living within that limbo space, but it is crucial to the life process.

When working with clients I have sometimes touched on these issues and have come up with my own set of guidelines as follows:

Guidelines for Change, Transition and Transformation

1. Take your time
It can't happen overnight. If you try to rush the process you will end up confused and therefore despairing of ever changing. There will be occasions where time seems to stand still and no progress is being made. If you have the courage to be patient and wait, you will find that this is the truly healing time, because you are providing space for it to happen.

2. Set yourself realistic but temporary structures
As you are moving through transition it is better to set temporary structures to live with for the time being. If you try to build permanent structures before you have completed the process, it will be more painful to deconstruct and you will be left with feelings of failure and low self-esteem. It may help to see the process as living in temporary accommodation (which is not ideal) while the

house you want is being built.

3. Let it happen

Although the spirit of willingness is essential to change, there is a strong tendency in a lot of people to make it happen by 'doing' instead of 'being'. Use the past as a resource and the future to organise without attempting to control too much. By staying 'in the moment' you can allow yourself to be spontaneous and be more in touch with what is happening to you. This can be scary as anything could happen but it also holds the rare beauty of appreciating the simple things that are happening right in front of you. These can be missed through over-activity and worry.

4. Choose friends wisely

Try to associate with people who are honest and accept you for who you are on a deep level. When someone is in a transition of change there can be a reluctance in some people to allow this to happen. There will be those who respond to your distress by trying to rescue you. This is your journey. No one can do it for you. There will be others who will block your progress because your changing is threatening to them. They may feel guilty and resentful because it pinpoints areas in their life that need to change. Stay true to yourself (whatever that may be) and only be with people who will support that.

5. Be good to yourself

Don't beat yourself up by setting up unrealistic goals and then feeling awful because you failed to achieve them. Celebrate small victories. Realise how far you have already come - this takes time and practice. Try to receive what people are giving you in terms of praise and support. If you are putting into practice Item 4 then you will learn a lot about how others perceive you. Having said this, it is also important to realise how you feel at any given time, regardless of the effect this may have upon others. You are the most important person in your life and it is other people's responsibility how they will react to you.

6. Learn to let go

This is the most frightening aspect of change and transformation, but the most crucial. Change is basically a death/rebirth experience. We have learnt, in our society, to fear death, but life cannot exist without it. You will be letting go and allowing to die a lot of old patterns. Allow yourself to grieve. Even if the things you are leaving behind are negative, they took up part of your life and will leave a gap when they depart. Don't be in a hurry to fill that gap. When we die we revert to the elements - the primal source. This is in essence chaotic but new life always comes from this source. You will be in touch with the Divine at its most basic at this point. Wait and listen. This is not the time for the linear thinking of ordered decisions. It will come in its own time. Otherwise you may replace your old patterns with some more subtle but equally tying regimes through panic.

Await your rebirth with courage and patience. It will come in the way that is right for you. Nobody's experience of this will be the same. This is your time. This is your journey. Good Luck.

These words are only guidelines. Find your own way to work through them.

I think personally that in the past, as well as being problem solvers, wisewomen and cunning folk were the counsellors of their time. Nowadays you can attain all sorts of certification in counselling skills, but observation has always been important within this craft, as I mentioned earlier. Reading the client is invaluable to my work. When a client lands on my doorstep, often I don't know them from Adam and haven't a clue what they want. The first thing I do is shake their hand. This gives me quite a bit of information. What does that physical contact feel like? I'm sure that you have shaken hands with people before and picked up all sorts of messages from that contact. Some are welcoming, some are reticent, and some are definitely repellent!

Next I invite them in to sit down. I note their body language, how they move through space. I then disappear into the kitchen to put the kettle on and wait for the small 'thump' which comes from upstairs – Mab is coming down to investigate! To deviate slightly, I had better explain that Mab is my cat and my familiar. Mab is pawing me as I write this so it seems appropriate to tell you more about her.

The circumstances of her birth were extraordinary. My friend's cat had a litter of kittens. One of these was born on Halloween, on the stroke of midnight. She asked whether I was interested in this kitten, and of course, given my profession said yes! So along came Mab.

When I acquire a cat, I always give it a kitten name to be going on with until its personality develops and

I choose its proper name. Mab's kitten name was Pumpkin. As she grew, she proved to be such a queen and was so Otherworldly, (she can walk the spirit world very easily) I thought her name should be Mab. It really suits her – Queen of the Faeries.

Mab is my familiar. Not every cat is a familiar, but it's a special relationship that can develop between an animal and a magical practitioner. One of the ways in which the familiar can work is to produce a peculiar mirroring effect. Several years ago I had a bad car smash – within days Mab got involved in a road accident also. I began to notice that when I had something wrong with me, she had something similarly wrong with her. Her behaviour mirrored mine. So, I've learned to watch her closely. The link can form like that.

She doesn't let people into the house if she doesn't like the look of them. She is a guardian and is very discerning with my clients. I have also done acts of healing for animals via Mab. So it does link with the old tradition in which witches were sometimes accused of 'sending forth their spirit via the familiar'.

A few years back, on impulse, I entered Mab in a cat food competition. (One of the prizes was a year's supply of cat food!) I wrote and told them about Mab's work as a familiar. After a few hilarious articles in the local papers, I was told that she had been short-listed in the Working Cat category. Well, the result was that she was runner up, which miffed Mab no end! There was no certificate, not even one can of cat food.

A lot of people expect Mab to be a black cat in accordance with tradition. The tradition they are referring to is more about the shape-shifting qualities associated with familiars. There are usually three types of cat that fall into this category. The black cat that merges with dark nights, the brindle cat that merges with most things, and the grey cat that merges with moonlight. Mab falls into the last type and incidentally also merges with granite, of which we have vast amounts in Cornwall. Mab is a wonderful companion as well as a working cat. The partnership has lasted thirteen years so far and I hope for many more years in the future.

It's interesting to watch the reaction between my clients and Mab. I also listen to the timbre and tone of their voice – how they string sentences together. All this information sets the scene for the storyline of this particular person. Incidentally this also makes every consultation relevant and personal to each individual. Sure, there are 'types' of people, but I maintain that everyone is unique, and I address each situation as such.

I am sometimes asked, cautiously, whether I read people all the time. Well, the answer to that is, yes unconsciously, but I do try and make sure I have my 'off-duty' times frequently – otherwise it would be overwhelming receiving all that information constantly. I trust myself enough to have faith that if I need to become more aware of someone's energies, then that fact will be presented to my consciousness and I will act accordingly. In the meantime, I keep these abilities for when I'm at work with my clients.

Below are some case studies, which will give a better overall idea of how I work with different people and situations.

One day I had a visit from a female client who had travelled from London for a consultation. This is always rather daunting when people are prepared to come from so far just to see me...well, you get out of magic what you're prepared to put into it. So many people say they are desperate when they come to see me. I'm not fazed when I hear that because I know that they've done the groundwork – they've tried all sorts of things to solve the problem. Also it puts them in the position of real willingness to be healed. I realise that it might seem strange to consider that people might not, on a deep and often hidden level, want to be healed. However, for some it is expedient to keep the status quo, in spite of going from healer to healer, and from workshop to workshop. You have to recognise when this is happening, otherwise it drains you very quickly. I've learnt to protect myself against this unconscious psychic vampirism, and to be firm in my dealings with these situations. However, this particular woman was very committed to her healing.

Her presenting problems were physical, involving a hormone imbalance. As I took the case history, I became aware that there was something quite fundamental to the problem that she wasn't revealing. This is always a challenging moment. My main aim is to enable empowerment in my clients, so pressure at this point is unwise, however, it was not possible to continue without this added information. I decided that this was the appropriate time to perform a tarot reading. I find this method effective at getting to the cause of the problem. Symptoms and life experience are but signposts to the root. Once the underlying cause is identified, then I search for the best way to handle it. Some say the Grail questions are, "What ails thee?" and "How may this be healed?" Well, I suppose that I work along a similar vein. What's the real problem that underlies the presenting 'symptoms'? And what's the best way to resolve the situation? So, it's fair to say that I regard the Tarot as a diagnostic tool.

As I laid the cards down it became immediately apparent that the root problem was connected with sexuality and shame. I gently asked my client whether she had experienced this in her life and the answer was in the affirmative and she elaborated. She then went on to say that she felt that she was being punished in the present for her past. From that point everything seemed to fall into place. I suggested that she was in need of a special purification or cleansing ritual in order for her to make a fresh start. She agreed to this and left for London, leaving me to arrange the ritual for a later date.

One of the first things I do when I am considering spells and rituals, is research to see what other practitioners have to say on the matter. It places me in the right headspace and psyches me up for the work in hand. Imagine my astonishment when I couldn't find one single example for a purification/cleansing ritual. Plenty for objects, none for people except to prepare for ritual. I found many rituals for cutting ties with the past but these were very dynamic and I instinctively felt that the ritual I was seeking needed a gentler approach. I was amazed by this discovery but also quite excited, and so I began the process of creating a ritual from scratch.

When I am unsure of how to approach a problem I try to identify the underlying energies. What's the overwhelming emotion here that is at the root of the problem? In this case - shame. Put simply, shame is a negative expression of an energy. What is the positive expression of shame? More research was needed!

Over the next few days I visited my friends (who I fondly call my tribe), and asked them what they thought the opposite of shame was. A tricky one, which made for some intriguing conversations. Finally we got it down to the closest being - glory. This was connected with references to auras and halos, which was part of what I was after, but still didn't contain that vital element I was looking for. We then tried 'glory' in the Thesaurus and a word appeared that created a deep resonance in me. The word was - lustre. I was immediately thrown back to childhood where I spent a lot of time prowling around museums and I knew/remembered that lustration was a holy ritual for cleansing. I looked the word up in the dictionary and, sure enough there it was, 'purification by ceremonial washing'. I knew that I had found what I was looking for. This wasn't a case for scrubbing or scouring - I wasn't after a psychic enema! Too many associations with guilt and shame for my liking. Lustration sounded wonderfully warm and inviting – a different type of spiritual cleansing that helped restore the client's self worth and esteem.

One of the more disturbing elements of sexual abuse is that one can be left feeling betrayed by one's own body. In my own experience, even though I knew with my mind that what was happening to me when I was younger was very, very wrong, my body responded anyway. This is an extremely confusing message to receive, especially at a young age. It can create a mind/body split that requires a special kind of healing. It also leaves shame and guilt by association and wariness about any response that borders upon sensuality. This is a toxic, deep wounding in the psyche and the body and needs gentle, warm cleansing and lots of TLC.

It became clear that cleansing alone was not sufficient. It would need tenderness and compassion for the self; a new healthier relationship between body and psyche, and this had to be in place before any other relationships in life could be addressed. I began to think of how I could set a sort of regime of self-indulgence and nurture of the body. Massage is always a good one, for not only does it feel wonderful physically, but also it gives the morale a boost. I encouraged my client to set aside every Friday to indulge in sensation function activities that were pleasurable. This all sounds a doddle to most people. Sadly, for abused people this is one of the hardest things to do. Since they are used to bad treatment they stay with what is familiar, because sensual feelings of any description can be overwhelming. This called for work with Aphrodite!

In my experience when there has been violation of the feminine, there are often problems with the womb, breasts and hormonal functions. It seemed appropriate to perform a ritual of rededication of the womb (the womb being symbolic centre of femininity). I found a version of this written by Caitlin Matthews and used parts of this which were useful for my purposes. It also became apparent that an important part of this ceremony would be that women attend the client. It was at this point that I knew that I would want to bring someone else into the equation. I wrote to my client asking her permission to consult with my colleague. I had a two-fold reason for this. Not only did I need another female attendant, but also my friend was a pellar. This is a Cornish word for a folk healer, and I needed her skills with herbs to address my client's physical symptoms.

Having gained my client's permission, we applied ourselves to the task of gathering information regarding appropriate herbs for the lustration, and for the alleviation of symptoms. All in all we managed to collect together some fascinating information on the whole subject. This has been invaluable as we both strongly feel that this ritual will be repeated in the future for a lot of people. I realised that I had discovered something important, not only for my client, but also for myself, and others who, through sexual trauma, had lost their sensual connections with their bodies. Unfortunately there are a lot of abused people out there and, to my knowledge, there is nothing in place, magically speaking, that addresses this issue.

The following case study is a good example of my approach to creating charms. Shortly after I became self-employed, a shop owner, who was suffering a spate of serious shoplifting and burglaries, approached me. He asked whether I could help him out and I immediately said that I was sure I could. It was only afterwards I realised that, at that time, I hadn't a clue what I was going to do! However, I have found over the years that this isn't an uncommon occurrence. The spell or charm seems to be most effective if time is given to just muse upon what to do, or letting the spell 'cook', as I refer to it.

So, I started to let my mind wander through various possibilities and I came up with the following thought processes. I took a pair of magpie claws, (association with thievery) which I just happened to have hanging around. (I am sometimes given the strangest objects, such as desiccated frogs, bones and such like, and you never know when they're going to come in handy!) I bound them to a cross of rowan (traditional protection image). Round this I placed a circle of ivy wrapped round with solder (both lead and ivy are sacred to Saturn which has a restricting energy). I made this charm and charged it on a Saturday (Saturn's day) at 10pm (Saturn's hour that day) during the dark of the moon (restricting energies). The charm was installed in the shop and acknowledged every day by the owner. This has been very effective, and I re-charge this charm every year and a day. At the time of writing the shop owner has informed me that this particular charm is still, "Working like a charm!"

When I create a charm I utilise materials that are 'in sympathy' with the effect required. Once gathered, I choose a time that is also compatible with the energies needed, and then I start working. Often the Child side of me comes to the fore when I am physically constructing a charm. The charms I create often appear quite primitive.

I feel that this is quite important to my work. Much of what I do activates, what I call, the primeval part of the human mind and makes a sort of race memory connection – just like an old forgotten memory of the Old Ways. Therefore, it shouldn't be too surprising to end up with an object that looks quite spooky or 'witchy'! Of course charms which are beautifully and carefully constructed, are no less effective – its just that primitive is the way that works best for me.

Once constructed, I charge the charm. This involves bringing the charm alive and kicking, and then instructing it regarding its function. Afterwards I usually place it on a special altar to 'simmer' for a while. (There are a lot of analogies between magic and cooking!) When I deliver and install the charm, I encourage the new owners to form a relationship between themselves and it. The best way this can be done is, as part of daily routine, to acknowledge the charm in some way. Some people find that giving it a name helps with this process. Many charms, but not all, require recharging after a certain period of time. This is not always apparent at the time of installing, so I usually wait to get feedback from the client.

When it becomes apparent with a client that it is important to effect closure, and although the mind understands this, the imprinted behaviour still continues with the old habit patterns; then this may well be the time to cast a spell. In these sorts of situations, a spell can be the kick-start that the client needs in order to move on with the rest of their life.

I have utilised the following simple but effective spell for release many times. In a sense, it's a way of tricking the unconscious into letting go of the painful connections with the past so that a fresh start can be achieved.

Carry around with you a notebook, and when so moved, write down all the feelings and emotions connected with what you're trying to let go of. This can be bereavement, the end of a relationship or anything that has passed its sell by date, so to speak. No one is going to read this apart from you, so really be honest with the expression of your emotions. I usually set up a propitious date, in this case a waning moon, on which to conduct the spell casting. These thoughts are written on pieces of paper, then folded up and kept in a ceramic pot– a terracotta flowerpot will suffice.

Once the appointed time is reached, then light a dark blue candle (for deep healing) and place the pot in front of you and empty out all the folded pieces of paper. One by one read them aloud. Then burn the papers one by one in the candle flame, letting the ash fall into the pot. So, you eventually end up with a pot full of ashes. By this time you will be feeling pretty emotional after reading how you really felt about the situation. For some people this may well have been the first time they have admitted to certain feelings. Build on this energy – really give it some 'welly' until you feel that you can't push any more energy into the pot. As the energy peaks – smash the pot! (It may be useful to keep something handy to smash the pot with – a largish rock or a hammer. Also have a cloth or some newspaper under the pot because you will be gathering together the remains.) Allow yourself to come down to earth slowly. This spell has a shock factor incorporated within it specifically as a dynamic device, so let yourself settle afterwards. Then, once recovered, collect together the debris and bury it somewhere away from the house where you live. When this is done, walk away. Do not look back. This is crucial. There are many stories and tales concerned with emerging from the Underworld (which is where you have been) and the importance of not looking back. Hence Eurydice and Lot's wife! This is symbolically very powerful.

You now have a fresh start. Go forward rather than turning back to old patterns. I usually encourage my clients to do something associated with fun the next day – like building a sandcastle or flying a kite! This particular spell has been very effective for many people, including myself.

And now, we'll have a look at cursing, or more to the point, the removal of curses. This is possibly the only situation where the witch or wisewoman is called upon over all others. Who else would you go to consult to break a curse? Deliverance ministry affected by churchmen is more concerned with cases of so-called possession after all – not quite the same thing, in my opinion. Helping people who believe they have been cursed is quite high on my list of reasons for consultation.

Ill wishing is a powerful force. The mind can produce thought forms and, if there is enough emotion, they can materialise. Quite frankly, if someone believes they have been cursed, they might as well have been – it has the same effect. Curses only work if there is a 'transmitter' and a 'receiver', in other words there is an unconscious collusion going on. My client is the receiver, and that's what I work on, for the client to stop being a receptacle for these negative energies. I attempt to clear the mind of the client from the 'Dennis Wheatley' images that have built up. Sometimes it's enough for the person to realise this and then they can change it, however a spell may be required from me to cut the connection. Even if this is the case, the client needs to do the groundwork to maintain non-participation in the previous collusion. When a curse is caste, if there is nowhere for that energy to hook into – that is, it is not picked up anywhere, then the energy goes straight back to its source – having picked up momentum on the way. A classic case of chickens coming home to roost! Due to this, one is advised to be careful in the issuing of curses and not to issue curses lightly.

I am very capable of cursing with the utmost potency, but like the Queen of Rods in the Tarot, just because I have a big stick, it doesn't mean I have to wave it around all the time. It's enough to know I have it. Certain women have what I call 'The Look' – I've yet to see it in a man. Before anyone accuses me of sexism, remember that absence of evidence doesn't necessarily mean evidence of absence! Anyway, regarding the Look. I'm sure we can all quote instances of this phenomenon – it's where a woman gives a look that stops people in their tracks. I remember Dame Janet Foulkes giving one of these looks in parliament many years ago – and I remember the reaction by the rest of the mainly male MPs. They squealed like young boys who had been caught doing something naughty! I also have this ability to stop things from going any further with The Look if I feel someone is pushing my boundaries. It used to be called the Evil Eye – and still is in many countries on the Continent. In short, it is far better to warn than to have a hair trigger as far as cursing is concerned. I have actually only cursed once, and that was more like a booby trap in its set-up.

The occasion was in response to a fire attack on two well known ancient monuments here in Cornwall – the Men-an-Tol and Lanyon Quoit. These landmarks are part of our ancient heritage and appear in many publications promoting Cornwall. The vandals concerned sent photographs of the monuments burning, together with a covering pseudo-occult letter threatening further damage to other sites within a week, to our local paper.

I thought long and hard about what to do in this situation, and decided that I would lay an anathema or curse around all the sacred sites in West Penwith. I made sure that this was made public by informing the newspaper concerned, and clearly stated that the curse would only be activated against anyone who was there with evil intent. For good measure, I incorporated within the ritual a search and detect element in order to track down the culprits. Now I realised that this was possibly a contentious thing to do, and predictably there were a few detractors to the issuing of the curse. However, given my role within the community, I felt that I needed to say/do something in response to this act of desecration and so took it upon myself to become pro-active. This is always difficult for people who prefer not to rock the boat, who tend to keep their heads down and hope it all goes away. So I came in for a lot of flack, but then it goes with the territory in my opinion! Incidentally, the outcome was that there were no further attacks on the sites, and the perpetrators were caught several weeks later and were successfully prosecuted. As always, I go by results and I considered the outcome successful.

Now, I'm not a historian – neither am I an anthropologist, although the subjects fascinate me. However, I wouldn't mind betting that most tribal communities in the past chose to celebrate definitive moments in their lives, known as Rites of Passage. Nowadays in the Western world we tend to only celebrate three main ones – Birth, Marriage, and Death – or Hatches, Matches and Dispatches, as I fondly tend to call them. Puberty rites and croning rituals seem to have fallen by the wayside, and when one looks at how our society views our youth and our elders, it gives pause for thought does it not?

Even when it comes to the acceptable rites that are performed, there is a sense of the 'conveyor belt' found within them. Happily more and more people are opting for rituals that are more personally meaningful. Whenever people approach me for a Rite of Passage, whether that be a Baby Blessing, a Handfasting (Pagan Marriage) or Last Rites, then I encourage them to create their own rituals. I basically act as stage manager to these events, offering suggestions and guidance where needed. Let me explain a little more about these particular rituals.

A Baby Blessing is as it sounds. Rather than initiating the infant into any particular religion, the gods (however the parents perceive that concept) are petitioned to ask for guidance and protection over the child, until it reaches an age where it can make its own mind up about what belief system to join, if any. The concept of godparents can be utilised with different friends and family members offering different gifts – what I call heart gifts. For instance, a close friend's child has a godmother who has offered the gift of adornment. She will help and aid my friend's daughter in clothes and make-up tips! I have also found within most of these ceremonies that I receive flashes of prophecy as I raise the infant up for blessing. The parents have told me that, so far, all these prophecies have been accurate. I often perform these rituals at a holy well, of which we have an abundance down here in Cornwall.

At the time of writing, Handfastings are not legally valid, but they are definitely spiritually valid. There is one concept that differs from what is on offer in society at present. Within a Handfasting, the couple take an oath to remain together as a couple initially for a year and a day. Then they review the situation and decide whether to remain together or not. If they decide to stay together, then the marriage lasts for as long as love lasts. If they decide otherwise, then a ritual of Handparting is conducted which releases the couple so that they can start new lives afresh. To me this is an eminently more sensible and realistic approach to something as sacred as marriage. Handfastings are also a brilliant opportunity to dust off the old besom, as 'jumping the broomstick' is a tradition that still remains and is generally a lot of fun!

During my many years in the nursing profession, I found that I seemed to have an affinity with the dying. In fact, I earned the nickname of 'The Angel of Death'! Terminally ill patients seemed to wait until I came on duty before they let go and died. And before the police start investigating further, I can assure you that I am not suffering from Munchausen-by-Proxy Syndrome! I seemed to work with ease within the whole process of dying and bereavement – not too surprising given all my Underworld experiences. Often 'wounded healers' have these types of skills. To be with someone as they die is a tremendously moving experience and a privileged place to be. Certainly there is a shift in energy at death as the soul departs the body. I've always felt that when people pass over, they end up where they want to be. For myself, I've had quite a few near death experiences and I've experienced a number of very vivid dreams about dying, so I have no fear of death itself but, like a lot of people, I'm concerned about the manner of my death. I believe that once one has passed this threshold that there is a time of rest in a place, which in the Craft is called the Summerlands – an evocative word. Then there is a choice whether one wishes to proceed with the next stage of the journey. Certainly I believe that the spirit or soul survives the body – it's just the form that changes. Neither do I see it as a judgement time.

It isn't about sin and redemption, but fate, which is a process of cause and effect.

I have connections with a group of people called the Soul Midwives. They are called upon to deal with all sorts of things connected with the death process: helping arrange a funeral, helping the relatives of the deceased, to mediate with a hospital to allow the body of the deceased at home, if they wish, to wash and prepare the body etc. So it has a very practical application as well as a soulful one where they sit in vigil with the dying. I also have worked with the souls of those who have passed over in distress and who are lost, I call it Soul Rescue.

Most people's ideas about funerals come from the Victorian era – black mourning dress, polished coffins, black hearses etc. After her husband Prince Albert's death, Queen Victoria led the nation in a lengthy and morbid outpouring of grief. Nowadays funerals are usually offered as a sort of package trip. Most people don't realise how much they can contribute themselves. Too many times peoples' nearest and dearest are handed over to strangers, so it's not too surprising to hear of stories where their dearly departed have been dressed inappropriately, or talked about in a way that doesn't connect with their memories of them. Some people prefer to just hand it all over to others because they are too upset to do otherwise, so a package deal suits them. However, I have found that others, who are prepared to put in that bit extra that personalises the ritual, have really benefited from the experience. Death is a life issue after all. Funerals are there for the living as well as the dead. Most undertakers are all too willing to listen to what the relatives want, and have come up with some quite inventive and creative ways of making the whole experience meaningful.

Death is one of the biggest taboos in our society, and many have a superstitious dread of discussing any sort of preparation towards it, and the subsequent depressing rituals reflect this fear of death. Yet, without death there would be no life. Any Last Rites ritual I perform is very personal and is a celebration of the deceased's life.

Obviously I need to meet with the relatives first and foremost. One of the first things I do is to remind them that there is no rush – there are no deadlines, if you'll pardon the pun. In this country there is not such an urgency to dispose of the bodily remains because we live in a more temperate climate. There does exist this tendency to get rid of the body as soon as possible, and although that is understandable from the point of view of removing that which is reminding people of the pain of their bereavement, it is much better to take your time over all the decisions that need to be made. Once they realise this, they can take more time to create a ritual that reflects the character and life of the deceased. In every case I make sure that there is plenty of space for anyone to contribute personally. This can take the form of an anecdote, a poem, playing a musical instrument – the list is endless. In this way everybody feels part of the ritual, rather than just one person speaking for everybody else. Taking part also helps tremendously with the grief process.

It's worth considering methods of body disposal, as there are many choices nowadays. Burial in a cemetery is still an option, although most of these places are run on quite military lines – rules about what one can write on headstones, all the graves looking the same with just grass and no mini-gardens anymore. Crematoriums raise questions of pollution and can be very impersonal, even though dispersal of the ashes makes for more flexibility. I was once asked to take the ashes of someone's mother

around her favourite supermarket and to discreetly
scatter them in the grounds of the car park – she loved
shopping there apparently! Woodland Burial is an up
and coming trend, which I heartily approve of. To me it
seems the most natural thing to be buried in the earth
where my body would feed a tree. Best form of recycling
in my opinion! Locally I have connections with the
Penwith Woodland Burial Place, and I already have my
plot booked. It's right by the gateway where I can be a
guardian to the site in the afterlife. It's got a wonderful
view over the countryside to my village. Why is a view
so important? Weird really, because I won't have eyes
to see it! However, I'm sure you know what I mean!
Every time I visit, I go and stand on my plot. It's an
extraordinary feeling, standing where you are going to
be buried – not unpleasant though – just strange.

In case it sounded like I was having a poke at funeral
directors – I'm not. There is plenty of scope to work
with the undertakers, because let's face it; some of
the services they offer are invaluable. It's more like
using what we need rather than having to take on the
whole package. As someone once said - it's a bit like
the difference between a package holiday, and a holiday
that caters to the individual. This is such a vast subject
that I recommend you consult the appendix for further
information.

On my website and within the leaflet describing my
work, it states;

> 'The main aim of my craft is to aid people in their search
> for healing, empowerment and fulfilment of their potential.'

Healing is a very general term that covers a multitude
of things. As far as I'm concerned, it's the starting point

for most people – after all, as a close friend of mine pointed out – we're all damaged goods.

Our society, sadly, in its over-adrenalised approach to life, has produced many forms of addictive behaviours. This is why a lot of my work is helping change old negative habit patterns. Although initially it may be a good idea to resist the addiction (whatever that may be – drugs, alcohol, relationships, food, sex etc) the whole purpose of healing is to reach the point where one can make an informed choice - so that you can indulge and not binge. Simply cutting things out that have caused trouble in the past leads to a very restrictive and denying lifestyle. It's about transforming the negative response into something more productive.

When I identify a repeated negative trait in a client, I ask what would be the positive expression of this energy? After all, it's two sides of the same coin. This means that whatever we have serious issues about in our lives, we hold within us the potential to be really good at it, once worked through. Therefore people who experience their lives as living nightmares have the ability to make their dreams come true... I firmly believe that the point of healing lies within the wounding. Often our addictions are a displacement activity in order to avoid looking at our wounds – and who can blame us, wounds are tender and raw, but it's not much good covering them up with sticky plasters, they'll just fester. I know enough as a nurse to realise that some wounds need airing and TLC to build up slowly the layers of healthy tissue.

When we have reached the point where we can freely choose what we want, and what we don't want, in our lives, then we have achieved empowerment. From this vantage point we can choose to live fulfilled lives – why put up with crumbs when you can have a banquet?

We know how to survive (otherwise you wouldn't be reading this, and I wouldn't be writing it!); this is about thriving.

Usually at some juncture in a consultation I ask my client whether they want to be healed. This is not as daft as it sounds, nor am I simply asking permission. I am attempting to evoke a self-healing response within that individual. I don't heal people – they heal themselves. How else can they attain empowerment - certainly not by me trying to do it for them? All I do is identify the options available, offer suggestions and choices. Then, when the client chooses, they take responsibility for those choices – even if they decide to do exactly as they have done before – it is still their choice, no one else's. When I do a Tarot reading, I don't ever tell my clients what to do. Readings are similar to a weather forecast – I might see that the energies are going to get a bit stormy, but it's up to my client to decide whether to push their boat out or stay in harbour.

Talking about boats and harbours, there's a brilliant quote on my bathroom wall. It goes, 'Ships in harbour are safe – but that's not what ships are built for.' Either way the client's destiny lies in their own hands.

I'd better explain about my bathroom wall...several years ago I had some structural work done in my cottage, the aftermath of which left the whole interior coated with rab dust. For those who aren't familiar with rab, it's a type of mortar used on a lot of old cottages down here, whose main constituent is earth. So, the result was everything was covered in dried mud! Much against my natural inclinations, I set to with gusto and spring-cleaned the entire house – giving the spiders 24 hours notice of eviction of course. (Incidentally this really works – so a handy hint for those of us who are sensitive to little creatures' lives.) This had the amazing effect of making the cottage seem much bigger and all the shadows had disappeared. "Jolly good thing too!" I hear some say. However, I found the extra light strangely disturbing and longed for the spiders to quickly weave new homes in order to soften the edges of things. The bathroom in particular was startling because of its now ultra bright white walls. This was unnerving for this little fish who felt very exposed in a place where they generally feel at home – Pisces being a water sign. I wanted the grotto type atmosphere back rather than this cold and clinical look.

Well, the point of this story is that one day I felt a very strong impulse to do something to the walls in the bathroom. I didn't have the money to get paint, and there was also the issue of time and energy. Feeling delightfully naughty, I grabbed a marker pen and started to write my favourite quote at that time on the wall. It felt that I had made quite a statement on an inner level because I got in touch with a little voice, (no actually it was quite loud!), that told me that I mustn't write on the walls. Too late! I had also got in touch with my Inner Subversivness and wrote boldly and with glee, then slammed down the pen with triumph. What I hadn't reckoned on was that the next person to visit the loo also decided to indulge the urge to write on walls – and so it continued to the present day. There are all sorts of diverse writings on my wall; some I don't claim to understand at all, and others have truly inspired me – as they have others. I find it interesting that many of my clients, if they visit the bathroom, find exactly the right quote they need. Incidentally, it also tells me a lot about them, depending on what their favourite quote was. I wonder if anyone has written a thesis on this desire in humans to write on walls? Maybe it's called the Graffiti Complex? It would make fascinating reading.

Finally, at least for this chapter, I want to talk about combining traditional methods with 21st Century tools. This sounds very straightforward but actually is a difficult concept to translate. Although there is documentation of cunning craft available, rarely does it reveal what they did in detail. There are descriptions of the type of work they performed, but unless any old books of charms are unearthed from attics, we have very little data on the recipes used. Much information about some aspects of cunning craft comes from old journals of granny's simples and potions, from old wives tales and folk medicine. Usually there is no mention of witchcraft per se; in fact lots of the remedies are applied with a prayer, to the four apostles for instance. However, this does connect with what I mentioned earlier with regard to utilising whatever is around, including religion. One place, which is ideal for the study of cunning craft, is the Museum of Witchcraft in Boscastle, Cornwall where they have many examples of artefacts connected with the Wayside Witch, as it's referred to. However, even here, there are little titbits of information, which are tantalisingly short. Enough to whet your appetite to experiment more I say! To say that I make it up as I go along sounds superficial, however, there is an element of truth here. I come from a stance of unknowing, then drawing on what I do know and what is unfolding, I move toward a knowing.

When I need to gain knowledge of a situation that is for now unclear, then I commune with the ancestors for the answer. Often this is about my work, but sometimes it's for personal reasons. I usually go for a walk in the countryside and ask myself what my predecessors would have done. I also walk with awareness as the natural world, (which includes the spirit world) can give me very clear and potent messages. I decided to go with my herbalist friend on a 'wisewoman walk'. As we sauntered down hedgerows, across sand dunes and along the beach, we immersed ourselves in wandering through the different environments. We also stopped for a smoke several times and talked about traditional ways. We agreed that tradition was essentially a handing on of material and information. Given that I have already mentioned the lack of detail available, my 'handing on of information' or tradition, has come directly from my relationship with the Old Ones and the spirit world. I believe this to be a valid heritage, however, I am certainly not saying that my way is the only way. It's a way that works for me.

When I ask the spirits for aid and they answer with just the right thing, I connect with a kind of old remembrance. I feel part of my tradition, not so much that I've learnt something new, rather I've remembered how to do it. Paradoxically it's often the first time I have tried a certain spell, and anyway, I usually have to update the method to fit into the 21st Century. Adaptation of others' spells is quite acceptable in my opinion. We need to continue to create new traditions, as some older ones are no longer relevant; in this way the Craft traditions evolve.

> "Do not follow where the path may lead;
> go instead where there is no path,
> and leave a trail..."

If things don't evolve, they die – and I'd like to have something to hand on. This brings me rather neatly to the question of an apprentice.

I feel that over the years I have built up a considerable

body of knowledge and experience about the Old Ways. I'd love to pass this on to a younger woman someday. I realise that my choice goes contra to Wiccan thought on the matter, who consider that this handing on should be from female to male or vice versa. (Unless it's a family member, when this law is relaxed. Not awfully sure I understand the thinking behind that exception... better ask a Wiccan!) However, if you look back at past documentation and artwork, nine times out of ten, you come across the image of a younger female apprentice who is depicted working alongside an old witch – you don't see young lads, except when they are shown with male wizard/magician figures. Besides which, I fail to see much point handing on female mystery magic to a bloke. However into his feminine he might be, he'll never know what it feels like to bleed, to give birth etc., so how can he utilise the energy? I'd be just as much at a loss if I attempted to perform male mystery magic. So it makes more sense to keep it in the family so to speak!

I believe that in the past, apprentices were taught the skills in exchange for other duties that the wisewoman found difficult, or couldn't manage anymore, and that's what I call Fair Trade.

In a more general sense I mourn the loss of apprenticeships in other professions. In my opinion there is no better way to learn a craft or skill than a hands-on traditional approach. Plus by removing apprenticeships we have in one fell swoop deprived the world of masterpieces. These were specific works of skill to show their prowess to their teachers. One could not become a Master of any skill without producing a successful masterpiece. Methinks that government has sadly thrown the baby out with the bathwater. Fortunately, this doesn't apply to the Craft of the Wise...

WISEWOMAN TALES

A few years ago, I was called out to North Cornwall to investigate 'strange goings on' in a lady's house. Psychic investigations of houses are always exciting, as you never know what you're going to find. Usually, I take along a notebook and write down the history of the place and the phenomena reported. I particularly make note of reaction from children, adolescents and animals, as these groups are especially sensitive. Often there have been structural alterations to the building, which can unsettle the home's energies. I've found over the years that the reasons for psychic disturbance fall into three main categories: Debris – Focus – Entity.

Debris is about the energies that build up within a house during occupancy. When you move into a new house, if you're lucky the previous occupants have cleaned up before they left. However, it is unlikely they have cleaned the house psychically. This means that the new occupiers walk straight into the last occupier's accumulation of energy – sometimes this is not a pleasant experience. However, this is quite simple to resolve with a cleansing ritual which I encourage the owners to join me in.

Focus is where someone is sending negative energy actively, although not necessarily consciously, towards the house. I attended a case once where a farmhouse had been sold out of the family, and family members were living down the road. They had a grievance towards the new residents since they felt their inheritance had been sold from under them. Focus is also seen when a house develops a bad reputation for any reason, this time the energy is fed by rumour and superstition. This is the realm of haunted houses and ghosts. In my opinion, ghosts and apparitions are impressions left behind after an event. The more dramatic or dynamic the event, the deeper the impression left behind. Often these impressions are absorbed into the materials around them, especially wood and stone. Nowadays this makes more sense when we realise that some of the properties of stone (graphite) are found in video and audiotapes, and that carbon dating techniques utilise wood to calculate time. So it's not too surprising to hear of the event replaying itself over and over in a haunting. Once again this can be sorted very effectively by setting up various charms and items that reflect back any adverse energies. It's always good to let the word get round after attending to a haunting, as then the superstition tends to die down as it's not being fed so much.

Finally entities. I have bad news for those who like melodrama and get off on sensationalist occult films. Entities are very rare. They do occasionally happen and I would deal with it or them in the way that was appropriate. However, many occurrences are mistakenly classed as 'evil' or 'demonic' when any of the above reasons are in operation, or there are psychological problems within the family set up.

To return to the 'haunted' house in North Cornwall; it was a large and rambling property and was the result of a conversion of two old cottages into one residence. There was an extensive garden which also had a dried up well by the back door. I listened as my client related events, which led her to wonder whether the house needed my attentions. There was a recent history of illnesses for herself, her two young daughters and all the animals in the household; problems with electrical equipment and plumbing; strange smells; problems with sleeping/nightmares; feelings of depression, lethargy and anxiety. I asked the usual questions of how long had this been going on for, and was there a significant event which may have sparked it all off. Apparently not. I then went to explore the house and grounds.

The first thing I do before setting out on the more pro active part of psychic exploration is, I find what I consider to be the heart of the house and declare my intentions to the house spirits. To me, a home is a living thing that is made up of a myriad of spirits, which often reflect the nature of the occupants, their experiences and the actual substance of the building. The heart of a building isn't necessarily going to be found at the physical centre of the house. Often it is found around the hearth for instance (not too surprising when you realise that the word 'hearth' comes from the same root word as 'heart'). Once permission has been sought and accepted, I raise the energy of the place by using a bullroarer.

A bullroarer is basically an aerodynamic object on the end of a long piece of string or rope. This object comes in a variety of sizes and materials – mine are wooden, leaf shaped and about eight inches long, and I have seen others made of ceramic and metal. The method is to twirl the bullroarer over the head until a humming thrumming noise is heard. This is the result of the object rotating rapidly and producing a strong sound vibration. It truly has an amazing effect on the atmosphere and really shifts the energy.

Once I have the house spirits' permission and

attention, I go exploring. Often I use a divination rod to aid me in this process – I can do it with my hands only, but it requires more effort. I believe I am at the age now where it's sensible to work for maximum output with the minimum of energy. In this particular house I found that the 'areas that needed attention' were mostly outside, with the exception of an area above my client's bed. The initial 'search and detect' having been completed, I sat my client down over a cup of tea and talked about what I had found. She went as white as a sheet, and then broke down in tears. She then related that there was after all, a traumatic incident in the recent past. All the areas I had identified as needing attention outside were where a woman, who had taken against my client in a very violent way, had spilled blood. This tirade had ended up with an attempted suicide by the well in the garden. The well had dried up since. This was going to be an interesting case! I reassured my client, performed a robust cleansing in and outside the house, and said that I would be back to install certain charms in the house, and to see whether the well could be healed. It was like the well had become some sort of barometer for the energies of the house. I knew that I needed more research into spells and charms regarding bloodshed – so I hotfooted it to the Museum of Witchcraft where there is an extensive library of all sorts of pertinent and interesting things to do with the Old Ways.

I'm very fortunate to have such a resource practically on my doorstep. I have spent many happy absorbing hours hunting for various spells and charms, and writings that have been collected over the years. I spent a whole afternoon researching and came away with lots of interesting ideas and information that would help in this particular situation. Then I returned home and put this information to good use by making a few charms and collecting certain herbs together.

One of the things I had come across when I was researching wells was that a traditional way of healing a well was to collect water from another, powerful well and to pour it into the ailing well. Since blood had been spilt, it felt appropriate to get some water from the Chalice Well in Glastonbury. The water from this is a reddish colour, having a high iron content, and thereby felt in keeping with what was needed. As it happened, I mentioned this to a friend of mine who was going to Glastonbury that weekend, so that worked out fine and felt auspicious. I also worked with the old idea of 'Tis not where water is a frog will be, but where a frog is water will be.' I had discovered that jasper and bloodstone were both connected to blood. So I purchased a jasper frog to sit by the well in the garden. The other thing I acquired was a hawthorn tree to act as a Guardian over the well. It was a very special little hawthorn as I had collected it from a site in the countryside that felt absolutely right. Once I'd got everything sorted out, I returned to the house and installed the house charms – one for over the hearth and one for over the lady's bed. Then I planted the tree, positioned the frog, and then poured the water into the well. I instructed my client to acknowledge the well every day and then left. It wasn't until several months later that I had any feedback from my client, but I was delighted to hear that almost immediately water began to appear at the bottom of the well. Since then the well has filled up completely and the energies around the house have changed significantly for the better. I gave a whoop of joy when I heard that! It's so exciting when that happens – when you attempt something that you've never tried before, and the whole situation takes you on a wonderful journey of exploration – and then the outcome is successful, which is the real icing on the cake!

Sometimes I am called upon to heal animals, and this was the case when a farmer from Devon contacted me to find out whether I could do anything for his horse, which was suffering from 'sweet itch'. Now I must admit that what I know about our equine friends could be fitted on a postage stamp! What I did was to contact a Romany and asked him about traditional treatments for this condition. He was excellent. He explained that the prevailing element here was fire – too much heat – 'hot blood' to be exact - and that I would need to work with cooling and calming the horse. Once again I did acres of research, something I really enjoy incidentally, and came up with the appropriate herbs and materials – I even came across an old Horse Whisperer's chant. I found that I had enough ingredients to make two charms, and did so. As the charm needed to be kept next to the horse's skin, it seemed a good idea to have a spare handy in case. I suggested that the owner wear the other charm next to his skin, forming a link with the horse. This had an unexpected result in that gradually the horse began to recover and his hair grew back, but his owner developed a very itchy rash all over his chest! He thought it a small price to pay if it meant that his beloved horse was getting better. Sure enough, after a few weeks the owner also recovered. Phew! However, I did learn something valuable from that, which is to acknowledge the bond between some people and their animals, and to be aware of this when performing any magic upon them. As far as I know, both client and horse are still healthy.

Since I have alluded to the Museum of Witchcraft

several times already, I thought you might like to hear a little more about this valuable resource we have in Cornwall. In 1960 Cecil Williamson created 'The Witches House', situated at Boscastle Harbour, Cornwall. In 1996, at midnight on Halloween, (I'd loved to have seen the solicitor's faces!) Graham King purchased the premises and he, together with his partner at that time, Liz Crow, transformed the interior into the accessible and educational museum that we have now.

I visited The Witches House many times over the years so have seen the radical changes as and when they happened. In those early days the journey from entrance to exit was strange indeed... let me take you through the experience. First of all you purchased your ticket from a veritable crone who sat in a tiny, ill-lit booth papered with red flock wallpaper. (Incidentally a small piece of this infamous wallpaper was immortalised in a frame which still hangs in the booth. Got to keep the purists happy!) You were given a ticket torn off a reel, identical with old cinema tickets; in fact you had the distinct impression that you were about to go in to see a seedy film! (Amusingly, the building was at one time a small cinema). Once inside you groped your way along dark, narrow corridors, which were lit only by the fluorescent light of the showcases. In these cases were the artefacts placed starkly against a backdrop of a colour, which can only be described as 'gabardine'. To me the whole place felt like 'a gabardine mac, which had rather dubious contents in its pockets'. You passed several tableaux, which had a definite Dennis Wheatley flavour! Postcards still exist depicting these sensationalist scenes. Finally, in the narrowest part of the building, were the poppets and curses – these do not make comfortable viewing in the best of circumstances - and from this intense energy you were plunged into darkness as you tried to find your way out. The way was barred by an intimidating figure of a Sorcerer who offered good luck at a price – in other words demanding money by menaces! At this point you reeled out of the place with a pounding head and usually made for the nearest pub for a well-needed drink! An experience indeed!

Nowadays it is still an experience, but less sensational and certainly more accessible and informative. My first contact with Graham King was in January 1997 when he phoned me. He wanted to know what ideas and changes Pagans in the area would like to see in the Museum. I suggested he attend our next Pagan Moot and hear for himself, which he did. Two main issues that came up were; the removal of the tableaux and a more dignified display of the skeleton of Joan Wytte. At that time she was hanging from a bolt in her skull within a cupboard for all to gawp at. We felt that she should be given a decent burial, and in time she was eventually laid to rest in a secluded place in the countryside and memorial stone was placed nearby. The members of Penwith Pagan Moot also gave crucial voluntary support with cataloguing the artefacts before the Museum opened at Easter that year. That was a memorable weekend!

Since the volunteers would be handling 'live' artefacts it was decided to perform a ritual before everyone arrived to effectively keep the artefacts dormant during this time. That was quite spooky I can tell you - walking around the Museum in the dead of night, binding hundreds of magical objects! I advised people to wear something reflective, or a small mirror. One person took me at my word and purchased a budgie mirror complete with little bell to wear in order to send back any negative energies! Very ingenious and effective. I was in charge of cataloguing, examining and packing the Curses section, so I had to deal with the infamous poppets. It was painstaking and cautious work – the last thing I wanted to happen was to be pricked by any of the countless sharp objects which most of these dolls contained! What struck me as I was examining these poppets was the incredible amount of detailed work that had gone into them. Many dolls were made from scratch complete with individual clothes, and in some cases, underclothes. One of the most disturbing poppets, who incidentally seems to be the ringleader when there's any trouble, had human hair under it's skirts... I can assure you that it was a very unpleasant experience finding that! So, a darker side to the adage that you get out of magic what you're prepared to put into it - the hatred that was coming off these poppets was tangible.

Once all the exhibits were safely boxed away, the transformation of the interior of the Museum could begin. Graham and Liz set to with gusto and installed proper lighting and appropriate backgrounds. I was asked my opinion regarding colour schemes to fit in with the different sections. For instance, black and red seemed very appropriate for the Curses and Persecution section. Purple, Silver and Dark Blue for Divination etc. Liz, having come from an Art and Textiles background, performed small miracles with a myriad of fabrics acquired from all sorts of sources, most being reclaimed. I think it's fair to say that the presentation of the artefacts in the Museum nowadays is far more accessible and is not trying to frighten the wits out of the general public – however, it remains thought provoking, and no apologies are made about the darker sections of the Museum. Some people have shown unease with the fact that one part of the Museum is given over to Satanism and Devil Worship, and that the

Curses and Persecution section remains. The reason for this is because it is a Museum and that this darker side needs to be present, because it is part of our history. No one wants to whitewash things, we leave the general public to make up their own minds, but at least they do that with the full facts.

As the Museum is privately owned, it cannot apply for funding, so the Museum is supported solely through the admission charges and retail of locally made gifts. Due to this the Friends of the Museum of Witchcraft was created. This runs under the same principle of League of Friends that operates within local hospitals. It raises funds from the membership and holds a Friends Weekend every winter, which is great fun. Just recently the North American Chapter of Friends has been started, so hopefully it will go from strength to strength. Funds from the proceeds go towards purchasing artefacts, equipment and materials needed to protect the many documents and books, which make up the extensive library. There will always be a need for this sort of thing so that the Museum can continue to function as a valuable resource for research into the fascinating study of witchcraft. Oddly and delightfully, I received in this morning's post a letter from the Museum telling me that I have been made an Honorary Member of the Friends for "always being there for the Museum". That was very heart-warming and timely to receive!

I know that I have mentioned before that a wisewoman's approach is to 'do the best you can with the materials available'. This next story is a prime example of that. One day I had a phone call from my friend and colleague, Penny. Penny is a remarkable woman who, together with her husband John, is responsible for the creation of the Penwith Woodland Burial Place. I first met Penny shortly before the Total Eclipse in 1999. I contacted

13. Full Moon at Lamorna. Photo credit: John Isaac

14. Magic meeting in the moonlight. Photo credit: John Isaac

15. Singing to the merfolk. Photo credit: John Isaac

16. 'When shall we three meet again…?'
Photo credit: John Isaac

17. Penkevyll the Lands End Obby Oss greets her Teazer (the Author). Photo credit: John Isaac

18. Teazing Penkevyll in the St Piran's Day procession in Redruth, Cornwall. Photo credit: John Isaac

19. Communing with the Land. Photo credit: John Isaac

20. Calling Spirit of Place. Photo credit: John Isaac

her about another matter, but it wasn't too long before I realised who she was as well. Over the years I had read of her endeavours to acquire Planning Permission for a Woodland Burial Site. Penny and John had set up a Pet Cemetery/Crematoria on their farmland, and in response to many requests from pet owners, wanted to create a site where humans could be interred with their pets. For various reasons planning permission was refused. We got on very well together and I asked whether she would mind if I worked some magic towards the next planning application, which was pending. She agreed, saying she was willing to try anything to get permission. It so happened that there was a meeting of the Penwith Moot that week so I asked people to link in with the magic. The planning permission was granted. This was great news and released a lot of ideas, one of which was to make a Lych Gate. Fortunately, I knew a craftsman who worked with wood who would love to make such an item. I put the two in touch with each other, Penny got the funding from a personal donation, and the work went ahead. Many months passed until I received the above-mentioned phone call, which was Penny asking me to come and consecrate the Lych Gate, as the workers were about to erect it. I quickly grabbed my coat, and dashed over to Rose Farm, where Penny lived.

It wasn't until I got to my destination that I realised that, in my haste, I had left my medicine bag behind. Now, I'm not saying that I can't operate without my equipment, because I can. Only I had built up a small collection of items that would be useful for most situations in my work. So I had to start from scratch and utilise whatever materials were to hand. An excellent chance to practise what I preach! The first thing I did was to visit the site where the Lych Gate was to be erected and just stood for a while taking in the atmosphere and getting in touch with the genius loci – spirit of place. This was an important structure we were creating, and it was crucial to perform a ritual that was in keeping with the energies in residence. I returned to the farmhouse and sat down for a cup of tea with Penny and began to formulate what I was going to do. I talked with Penny about how I believed that formerly some sort of sacrifice or appeasement was performed whenever an important edifice was erected. In more primitive times the sacrifice was loss of life of some description, however, nowadays this needs to be adapted somewhat according to our sensibilities. It was quite an interesting talk, and there was part of me that was sitting back and listening to what I was saying. I get like that sometimes – my friends call it 'going off on one'! Anyway, I asked Penny whether she was willing to make the sacrifice of... four eggs. As Penny runs a well-stocked farm of much loved animals, this was no problem. She immediately disappeared and returned with four, still warm, eggs. She informed me that the eggs were fertile, which seemed even more in keeping with the concept of sacrifice. I then went away on my own and spent my solitude conjuring up some sigils to write on the eggs. Sigils are simply abstract, drawn symbols, which act as a seal for the Magical Will. Sigils can represent complex concepts, but on this occasion I felt it was more beneficial to keep things simple. So I created sigils for the four elements – earth, air, fire and water. I then inscribed these sigils on the four eggs in red ink. Together, Penny and I placed the eggs in a small basket nestled in amongst some appropriate herbs I'd gathered from the farmland, and made our way up to the burial ground.

My friend, who had made a wonderful job of creating

the Lych Gate, was there supervising a small group of blokes who had just finished digging the holes for the posts. They backed off for a fag, and stood watching as they leant on their shovels. The actual ritual was very low key to observers – I simply asked for acceptance from the spirits as I went round the four postholes and smashed an egg in each hole. However, for me it was extraordinarily potent. I was acutely aware that as I smashed each egg, I was quite literally killing something – and that added a tremendous boost of energy. Penny did tell me later on that the eggs would have been eaten anyway, however, my apologies to any vegans who may be reading this! The Lych Gate was then erected as we watched, and I felt very much in touch with a sense of sisterhood and tradition. It felt really good to have produced a simple and effective way to consecrate something, intuitively utilising wisewoman skills. I have since revisited the site, and the Lych Gate has undergone a marvellous transformation. It appears to have completely merged itself with the surrounding Cornish hedge – it looks like it has grown out of the hedge, so it fits perfectly with its environment. If you ever visit the Woodland Burial Place, take some time to sit in the Lych Gate and soak up the energies there – I think you'll find it a remarkable experience.

Whilst mentioning Penny, it reminded me of a distinctly 'spooky' experience, which demonstrates the potency of image magic. Among her many skills, Penny is a gifted sculptor. Her speciality is making bronze heads. Many people have modelled for her, including myself. During the process of making the clay representation of me, Penny discovered that the work had developed a fatal flaw and had to be deconstructed. When she nonchalantly told me this over the phone I had a very strong reaction in the pit of my stomach. I asked her when she demolished the head and she was able to tell me exactly. As I had feared, at that precise moment I had received some startling news that 'really did my head in'! Well, that made me think, I can tell you! I've subsequently spoken to quite a few artists who are very aware of the sensitivity surrounding portraiture and are cautious as a result. No wonder tribal folks generally balked at having their photograph taken because they were afraid of their soul being taken away. I tend to stay well clear of image magic for this very reason. I hadn't given a thought to what might happen when I agreed to have my head sculpted – but I am very aware now, and so is Penny! Another lesson learnt... and so it goes on. I learn something everyday, in fact I believe that when people say, "I know" all the time, they stop learning. Even if I know a fair amount about something, I will still ask what other people's point of view is. They may come up with something different, which can shed new light on things. An open mind and an open heart are crucial to this work, in my humble opinion.

Occasionally I am called upon to help small children. This is nearly always a rewarding experience. Most children's minds are very open to magical experiences, and this makes the process much simpler and more straightforward. A case in point was as follows: One day a mother and her six-year-old daughter visited me – let's call her Jenny. The problem with Jenny was recurring nightmares, which meant that she inevitably ended up in her parents' bed for the night. This had been going on for almost a year, and although many things had been tried to break this pattern, nothing had worked. So, I sat down and talked with Jenny and found out that the bad dreams had started after watching something scary on the TV. This image had quite literally haunted her ever since. After hearing the story I said to Jenny that we were going to do two things. One – we were going to do a spell to make the bad dreams go away, and two – we were going to make a special charm, which would protect her while she slept so that it wouldn't happen again. Jenny and her mother agreed and listened carefully to the instructions.

Firstly they were to buy a helium balloon – it didn't really matter what pattern – that was up to Jenny. Then they were to obtain a tie-on luggage label. On this label Jenny was to write the thing that she wanted taking away – in this case, bad dreams – and to then sign her name. This label was then to be tied to the string of the balloon. Finally they were to take the prepared balloon to a high hill in the nearby countryside and release it. As the balloon sailed away, so her problem would go with it. It was important to watch the balloon until it disappeared from sight. This can take quite a while but adds to the focus of the spell. The last thing to do was to turn around and, without looking back, make their way home for tea. End of part one.

Part two was to make a charm for protection whilst asleep. What I had in mind was to create a 'filter' to hang over the bed. Seeing that dream catchers are very popular I decided to work with this image. As I'm a great believer in 'knitting your own' rather than buying ready made, I asked Jenny whether she was interested in making her own dream catcher. She was very eager to do so – happily Jenny already had an interest in making beaded jewellery and was quite dextrous. I gave her instructions how to simply create this, and also lent her one that I had to be getting on with until she made her own. Her little face lit up at the thought of borrowing a witch's dream catcher! Many months later I bumped into Jenny and her mother at the Mazey Day festival in Penzance and they told me that it had all worked a treat.

That was very satisfying to hear. It's always good to get feedback, and the thank you cards that festoon my cottage bear witness to how my profession has helped many people.

A significant part of my work involves wart charming. It's interesting that this is an ability that a lot of people have and is often passed on through the family. There are so many different methods of achieving this that one could write a whole book on this subject alone. Over the years I have experimented with many techniques and now I find that I automatically know which approach to use with each client. Let me give you a few examples. Some swear by rubbing the warts with some sort of biodegradable substance – a piece of meat, potato, bread etc and to then bury it until it rots. The thinking behind it, which is basic sympathetic magic, is as the substance decays so the warts disappear.

Then there is the infamous 'get lost box'... I use the word 'infamous' because this method is a throwback to traditional folk magic. Into a small box are placed some small objects which are representative of whatever the operator wishes to banish – the box is then wrapped up carefully so that it resembles a small package. This is then left at a crossroads until someone passes by and out of curiosity picks it up. The theory is that the 'complaint' is then transferred to this person. So beware of small enticing looking packages left at crossroads!

Now because I find this approach a bit dubious, I have adapted it to suit the times. I would use some tiny pebbles or small balls, plasticine works quite well. I place the same amount of objects as the warts into the box. I use matchboxes rather than make the parcel look tempting and eventually these disappear, probably into the nearest rubbish bin – but no matter – the important thing is that the spell randomly gets moved on. I believe that movement is crucial in spellworking – after all magic is by its nature pro-active. I see no need to deliberately focus on transference – I let fate take its course.

Often I buy the warts from people so that they become my property – the going rate is a penny per wart. I then ask for a drawing of the part of the body where the warts are. So, if they are on the hands – draw round the outline and mark each wart with a small cross. I then ask for the client's signature and a small lock of hair as contact items. Then at a propitious time – waning moon is good – I perform whatever wart-charming spell feels appropriate. Now, so far I have been working with alleviating symptoms, so we need to address the cause. In my many years as a wisewoman I have observed distinctive patterns regarding acquiring warts. Although the general belief is that warts are associated with old women, by far the age group most likely to develop warts are youngsters. Usually the peak occurs between puberty and young adulthood, roughly 11yrs – 20 yrs. It is highly likely that hormones have a part to play here, however, I have found that in all cases there is something in the life of the client that is causing feelings of intense frustration and powerlessness. This is probably from where we get the term 'worry wart'. If this is not addressed, then even if initially the warts disappear, they will return because the cause has not been resolved. Obviously it depends on what the particular underlying problem is as to how to resolve it. In many cases physical exertion is a key to the healing, particularly if it is creative as well. It's all that dammed up energy that's squeezing warts out; so pro-active expression moves it on and through. It's interesting work and to be honest I'm not sure why these odd little spells work – but they do. After all I don't have the kind of mind that has to know how things work – I'll leave that to inventors and scientists – I'm more interested in results. If it works, I'll probably use it no matter what.

Another area that has produced discernable results is simple Tarot reading. I was taught years ago that every witch needs to develop some form of divination. It doesn't really matter what form this takes, in fact it's a really personal thing. I was fortunate in realising quite early on that I was attracted to Tarot and set about learning all I could. I swiftly found out that purely reading books was not sufficient. I started to sleep with a different Tarot card under my pillow each night and documented the effect this had on my dreams. I found this very useful – until I tried the Wheel of Fortune card... my head was spinning so badly that I felt nauseous and had to take the card away! I found that I had a breakthrough with Tarot reading when I decided to go out on a limb and work intuitively. I picked a friend who I knew would be completely honest with me and 'read the cards' for her. Apparently the reading was amazingly accurate, and I went from strength to strength, backing up the intuition with the groundwork of reading traditional meanings as well. However, it's one thing to do a reading for a friend, and quite another to do the same for a total stranger. It requires faith and confidence in your abilities as well as a keen sense of responsibility to your client. By this I mean that it is irresponsible to suggest to a client that certain things will happen to them no matter what. As mentioned previously, I see Tarot readings as similar to weather forecasts – which are conjectural estimates of a future event. It's not my job to tell my clients what to do, but I do offer them all sorts of options. In this way I am not disempowering my clients, but encouraging them to make their own life decisions – for better or worse. I also do not hold back information of what I see in the cards – I am always honest with them. However, I do give careful thought to how I deliver that information responsibly. Often I have no idea what people do with the guidance that comes through a Tarot reading, but occasionally it unfolds before your eyes and that can be a bit unnerving! The following story illustrates this:

Several years ago I was approached by a woman who was related to someone I know in the village that recommended me as a Tarot reader. She was on holiday and requested a reading before she went back home. The reading plainly showed that there was an attraction to another man who was not her husband. This occasionally happens and is always a dodgy moment, but I gently suggested this and it was found to be true. When I mentioned that this attraction was mutual I saw her whole face light up. I knew with a sense of inevitability that this would be acted upon – and it was. This is when the whole weight of responsibility can bear down on you. Over the next few months I was informed of the upheaval that occurred as a direct result of my reading. I don't think my village friend was too pleased with me at the time because of the disruption, but eventually my client left her abusive husband and took up with her new lover. Fortunately this new relationship was successful and they now both live happily together not too far away from where I live. I met up with the pair of them quite recently and they both thanked me for bringing them together and for their fresh starts in life. Phew!

Most people at some point in their lives have to deal with the problem of bad neighbours – unless of course they are very fortunate! Sometimes all that is needed is common sense and self-assertion to resolve the situation, but sadly some people's lives are made a misery to the point where their health is affected by the 'Neighbours from Hell'... this where I occasionally get called in to help. I always visit the client in their own home, if at all possible, so that I can get a clearer picture of what's going on. Then I listen to the stories, with back up from third parties if possible. (Sometimes it can be six of one and half a dozen of the other!) I may perform a Tarot reading about the situation, but often this just confirms the information that I'm already picking up intuitively – but it's good to check these things out further if unsure. Generally I perform a Reflective Shield spell, which works very well with chronic, long-standing situations. The essence of this spell is to 'Return to Sender' any energies that may be directed towards my client. In this way any negativity is sent back to source and believe me, very few people are happy with receiving back their own negative energies, as it seems to pick up 'interest' on the way back. As a local saying goes – what goes round comes round. I also like this method of resolution as it contains the possibility of the instigators, on reflection, changing their attitude as their behaviour is mirrored back to them.

Some of the results of this sort of magic have been startling and such was the case for a woman whose private space was constantly being invaded by her intrusive neighbour. The last straw for my client was that next door's cat seemed to be acting out her owner's behaviour by digging up plants and generally befouling the area. After the spell was performed, not only did the neighbour stop being a problem but also my client noticed something else. The very next morning she watched the cat approach the boundary of her garden with its usual swagger, only to stop in its tracks suddenly – laid its ears back and turned tail and ran away!

I also have a spell for emergency situations – and by emergency I mean if someone's life is in danger. I can perform a binding spell, which has the effect of stopping someone in their tracks before they can harm anyone. However, I rarely resort to this as I am effectively exerting my will over someone else and this goes against my ethics. Also I see a binding spell as similar to the action of a tourniquet – it can't be left for too long before it would cause harm. So I only utilise this so that my client has time to remove themselves from immediate harm.

Over the years I have utilised many, many spells to help others. These have come from various sources. Although some have come from the past, i.e. old traditional charms and spells and a lot are made up 'on the hoof' so to speak, a sizeable amount have come from other practitioners who are willing to pass on their experiences to others. I personally have found that the most effective spells are the simplest – maybe that's why some of them are called 'simples'. This is not to say that more sophisticated and complicated spells do not work, because they can and do. However, I feel it is important that the practitioner is comfortable and confident in their method and approach to magic, and I get best results from simplicity. With this in mind I want to tell you about an interesting spell for finding lost objects. It's referred to as 'Pinning the Devil' and is probably given this title as a reference to mischievous house spirits. I first came across this in a book several years ago, but have also heard report of it by word of mouth locally. It sounds like it falls in the category of an Old Wives' Tale, but is surprisingly effective.

One day a few years back, I had an agitated phone call

from one of my friends. Her partner was due to leave the next day for Australia to rush to the side of his ailing father – and they couldn't find his passport. They were at their wits end and had searched high and low through their house, which was a considerable size, so lots of places for the passport to hide in. I gave my friend details of the spell, which she performed immediately. The next morning, with only hours to spare, the passport fell out at their feet from a pile of papers on top of a wardrobe. Interestingly, where the passport fell was in direct line with where the spell was set up. This is a fascinating pattern I have observed with this spell, that it appears to be geographically connected. I had occasion to call upon this spell when I was trying to hunt down a chequebook that I needed for my accounts. Directly underneath where I had anchored the spell I found what I was looking for!

I'm going to finish off this chapter by telling you about my travels as a wisewoman. The last thing I thought I would be doing, given my low income, was globetrotting! It all started a couple of years ago... I happened to be in Boscastle visiting a client and so, as usual, I paid a visit to Graham King at the Museum of Witchcraft. He had two Americans visiting him, one of who was a Professor in Religious Studies based at Indiana University. Graham recommended that they speak to me as a modern proponent of the art so to speak. So we trundled off to the nearest pub where I was subjected to many interesting questions about my profession. After a while Terri (the professor) turned to her companion and said that my approach to my work sounded very similar to Marilyn Johnson's - an Ojibwa Medicine Woman that she had worked alongside for many years. Would I like to meet her? Would I? Yes please!

Over the following months arrangements were made

for Marilyn to visit me in Cornwall. I had no idea what to expect as I had quite deliberately declined to get swept up in the fashion of 'Native American' spirituality. I felt that the tribes of the Americas had suffered enough without Western culture purloining their sacred rites and rituals. I know that's a rather contentious stance but that was my personal choice on the matter, and I certainly don't condemn sincere people who sensitively utilise these themes in their work. It's not their fault that there are a lot of rip-off merchants out there in the realm of spirituality. However, my bottom line is: it's OK to share someone's hearth fire for a while, but it is far better to find your own hearth. In other words, look back into your own traditions where possible rather than taking others' traditions. So, off my soapbox and on with the story.

When Marilyn and I first met, we were both relieved to find that we were dressed in ordinary clothes. I know that sounds odd, but we both had concerns about how we would look. Was Marilyn going to be bedecked in beads and dream catchers – and was I going to be dripping in amber and pentacles, not to mention crushed velvet! We spent several days visiting different places of significance including a fine example of a replica Iron Age Roundhouse that had been created on my friends' farmland. It was good to show Marilyn that my ancestors also lived in circular dwellings, although they couldn't be dismantled and moved like tepees!

Within these wanderings we found space to have our conversations documented. This was quite important, as ultimately our discussions would be used as material for a book that Terri would edit. It was fascinating to compare and contrast our approaches to our work, but I'm not going to go into any more detail about this now. You'll have to wait until Terri's book is published!

Suffice to say, I thoroughly enjoyed meeting with another traditional healer and felt acknowledged and uplifted by the whole experience.

The following year I visited Marilyn in her homeland of Ontario, Canada. This was a huge adventure for me. I had never flown before – (well, not by aeroplane anyway, too far for a broomstick!) – and here I was travelling halfway round the world on my own. I found that I was totally exhilarated by flying, especially once the plane flew above the clouds. What a truly beautiful sight! I spent the whole eight hours glued to the window and found it extraordinary that hardly anyone on the plane was taking any notice of the panorama outside and had their heads stuck in books, magazines and videos. My visit to America was marked by my sense of wonder about practically everything I experienced. I wasn't prepared for the temperature difference when I first stepped outside of the airport at a stopover at New York. Since smoking was not allowed within the airport's precincts, I nipped outside and it was like being enveloped by a hot, clammy blanket. I rolled a damp cigarette (I was going to say, fag, but I learnt very quickly that this word had a completely different meaning in America!) and watched the world go by. And what a strange world it was. I've always been a country girl and rarely visit cities, and here I was in noisy and bustling New York of all places – a far cry from the wilds of rugged Cornwall! As I stood there a stretch limo purred to a halt in front of me. I'd only ever seen these things on film and wasn't prepared for how big they are. This one was at least three car lengths long and seemed to go on forever. I was expecting some movie star to emerge from within, but it was just an ordinary family with children in t-shirt and shorts – how disappointing, and what an odd way to travel. What on earth did they do with all that space in the middle – play tennis? As I had a five-hour stopover until my next flight, I re-entered the airport complex and spotted a sign marked 'Rest Room'. Great! I had visions of a lounge with easy chairs where I could put my feet up for a few hours. I was sadly disillusioned to find that this is the American version of the public conveniences! After many uncomfortable hours perched on plastic seats, I eventually caught my flight to Pittsburgh and met up with Terri.

I went on to have many adventures during my stay in Pennsylvania and our subsequent journey to Canada, a lot of which was caught on film as a kind friend lent me their camera so that I could keep a video diary. Suffice to say that I had a fantastic time meeting up with Marilyn and her family and was shown many sacred things connected with her tribal traditions. What an adventure, and all for free!

Canada is a beautiful country full of trees, rocks and lakes. It's good to know that there are still places of wilderness and spirits. One place in particular I felt this power of sentience – it was called Dreamers' Rock and was found at the northern approach to Manitoulin Island, which is the largest freshwater island in the world. This is a sacred place of pilgrimage for the Ojibwa, or Anishnaabe, as they are known locally. The function of this rock was that, after climbing on top of it, the seeker would spend nights sleeping there until they received their spirit dream that foretold their destiny. This was no mean feat, as I discovered that the sleeping platform was in a very high and precarious position. In order to visit Dreamers' Rock a permit had to be obtained from the White River First Nation office, as any visitor had to be accompanied by an Ojibwa. After some considerable climbing and scrambling through forest and rocks, we emerged at the foot of Dreamers' Rock.

I was mesmerised by the stunning views, and the air was alive and crackling with energy. Marilyn climbed to the top of the Rock up what appeared to be a sheer face, and encouraged me to follow her. Fortunately I used to be a rock climber so this didn't present me with too many problems, and I soon worked my way up the rock face until I was just below the platform. Then I stopped. It didn't feel right to go any further. As soon as I realised this I heard a croaking noise very close to me. On looking up I saw two ravens swooping down and around us. This was a magical moment for me as raven had been a powerful guardian animal for me for many years. I decided that I would descend from the Rock and as soon as I reached lower ground I heard Marilyn call out. I looked up again and saw that an eagle, a bald eagle to be exact, which was circling and mewing around Dreamers' Rock, had replaced the ravens. This excited Marilyn, as eagle represented the Great Spirit and was considered to be very auspicious. I felt very emotional and honoured by my visit to this magical place, and I will never forget it.

Another thing that I found very inspiring and powerful was the native art and craftwork. For many years such things were denied to the native people, but in the last decade or so there had been a renaissance in this work. To begin with their art and crafts had been marketed by white men with a percentage of sales being passed on to the native communities. Fortunately and just recently, the Ojibwa had been granted permission to open their own galleries and retail outlets. This was something to celebrate, as their artwork is truly inspiring and their craftsmanship is exquisite. Most of the materials that they utilise are natural and indigenous to their area - like cunningly made birch bark boxes which had porcupine quills woven into them. I was able to purchase a few examples of their work to bring home with me, and I treasure them.

I had often wondered whether there were people in other countries and cultures who did the same sort of work that I did – albeit called by different titles. Certainly this was the case with the Ojibwa – was I going to get the chance to explore this theme again? Well, someone up there must have heard me because within a few months I was off to Africa!

Now I can't go into details about the whys and wherefores of this trip because of confidentiality issues, but it did involve some very potent workings. When you are within another culture you can't just impose your own form of magic – you have to work with what's already there. Interestingly, whilst I don't usually remember my dreams, in Africa I found I was having very vivid and instructive dreams which involved what I can only call Night Battles. However, what I can talk about are many interesting adventures I had during my stay.

Africa is still a wild continent in many ways and there was a lot of civil unrest due to a general election whilst I was out there. It was commonplace to hear of ambushes and murders in the locality, and it was necessary to be vigilant at all times – both with the populace and the wildlife. Aids was rife, and there was appalling poverty and corruption that sat very oddly with the vibrancy and exoticness that surrounded me. Danger within Paradise indeed! If I thought it was hot in America, then at least I was semi prepared for the intensity of the temperatures in Kenya – all without air conditioning. I observed the locals and noticed that they hardly ever moved at speed, but sauntered along and stayed in the shade when the sun was at its zenith. I learnt to do the same and to keep my head covered at all times when in the sun. The first thing I noticed was the brightness of the stars at night and the strangeness of the moon. It appeared much larger, and whereas in Britain the moon as it increases and decreases has its horns to the side, here the moon as it rose had its horns pointing down and by the time it was close to setting had its horns pointing upwards like a crescent shaped boat. I suppose this was because it was very close to the equator. I stayed in small huts called bandas traditionally made of mangrove poles and palm leaves with windows, which were open to the elements. There were some very strange noises at night from the various creatures that scampered across the walls and floors. I had to consciously keep my fertile imagination in check in this wild land where there were no cars, street lighting, electricity or running water.

One of my most enjoyable experiences there was to go snorkelling, which I had never done before. I took to it like a fish to water. What met my eyes was stunning. It was like swimming in an aquarium with the many coloured and exotic creatures that swam in and out of the many coral reefs. Many was the time that I had to pinch myself so see if I was dreaming this. My body was prepared for winter, yet here I was in the tropics a long, long way from home with its mists and sea breezes.

The magic here was very different – it was primitive, unpredictable and challenging. I met witch and bush doctors whose sometimes dubious practices could be bought, but I still hadn't met the type of traditional healers that I wanted to connect with – this was to come later on in my trip when I met the Maasai people. It came about through good networking via a good friend who I was travelling with. She had made friends with a Maasai woman who had connections with people in a township called Narok. Reaching Narok in the first place was quite an achievement. We had bought tickets in Nairobi for the journey, and through a series of misadventures, found ourselves squeezed into a battered old saloon car that was meant to hold no more than five people – there were nine people in ours! There then followed the scariest journey I had ever undertaken...

I was squashed against the back left hand door that didn't lock properly, and because they drive on the left hand side of the road, was frequently subjected to views of horrifying drops, especially when we careered down the Great Rift Valley. I say, careered, because the average speed of the vehicle seemed to be 100 miles per hour! It was truly terrifying and I was wondering whether I would survive the journey. Eventually the road turned into a track with huge potholes and the car seemed to spend most of its time at a 45-degree angle, tilted towards my side. It sounded like the exhaust was about to part company and I had visions of being stranded out in the bush at the very least. Eventually we rolled into Narok where we literally fell out of the car exhausted and traumatised. Fortunately we found our contact relatively easily and were soon established in a small hostel on the edge of the town.

Thanks to our contact, an appointment was arranged for us the next morning to visit a Maasai elder called Moses who lived and worked just up the road to where we were staying. Our subsequent interview with Moses was very successful. He was a renowned hereditary healer who had some fascinating tales to tell us. Apparently there is a special tribe of healers within the Maasai who live in an area called evocatively, the Forest of the Lost Child. This was where Moses' home was when he wasn't working in Narok. He could only spare us an hour then, but later that evening came round to see us at the hostel where I was able to speak more freely about the sort of work that I did. Moses said that in his culture I would be known as a Labon, which is their term for a traditional healer who worked within the community. I was well pleased with this contact and so we decided that we would like to go on a small safari before we went home and we made our way to Lake Naivasha.

We stayed in a delightful place called Fisherman's Camp on the shores of the lake. It was quite lush with lots of trees and interesting wildlife such as monkeys, ibis, multi-coloured birds, and at night – hippos! The next day we found Hell's Gate National Park where we found we could ride bicycles in the park. Obviously there were no lions, but we didn't mind that. It was extraordinary to be cycling through dramatic scenery were there were zebra, giraffes, baboons, and wart hogs in the bush and running across the road. We noticed in the brochure we were given that there was a Maasai Cultural Centre and we slowly made our way towards this. We imagined that we were going to some sort of refreshment point where there would be Maasai selling goods and crafts. What met our eyes once we made our way over the top of a hill was very different to what we expected. It was a working Maasai village called Oloorkaria.

Maasai villages are constructed with all the huts in a circle and thorns surround the perimeter. This means that they can keep their cattle safe within the boundaries at night. It's worth mentioning that cattle is the Maasai's currency and a Maasai warrior cannot marry until he has acquired a certain amount of cattle for the bride price. As we entered the village we were met by the Headman who introduced himself as Charles. All the men gathered round and proceeded to demonstrate Maasai singing, dancing, weapon throwing and fire making skills. It was fabulous watching them – the Maasai people are very handsome, colourful and dignified. After this we were shown the crafts they made including spears, knives, pots, gourds and beautifully intricate bead jewellery. Whilst we were involved with this, Charles pointed towards me and asked what I had hanging around my neck. For many years now I have worn a pendant/amulet that I made which contains a piece of coral with a hole in the middle, from which is suspended an obsidian arrowhead, a seed pod and a piece of Cornish slate. I explained what the pendant was made from and its protective use. Then on impulse I showed Charles my bullroarer that I had bought with me, explained its use and asked permission to demonstrate, which he agreed to. It was a fantastic experience to twirl the bullroarer in a Maasai compound – the acoustics were amazing! Not too surprisingly this attracted a lot of attention from the others and the women and children, who had kept to the background, all started to gather round in interest.

Next we were taken into one of the huts, which were small, dark and cunningly made. It so happened that I found myself in one of the rooms alone with Charles. He said to me "I knew as soon as you entered our village that you had powers. And the reason I know you have powers, is because I have these powers too." He then extended his hand towards me in greeting. The handshake was slightly odd which involved linking thumbs, but I'm darned sure it wasn't Masonic! Well, you could have knocked me down with a feather – that really blew my mind. I couldn't stop grinning!

Unfortunately time had run out and we had to leave, but before we did I was asked to leave my name and address on this form along with any email address. I didn't notice a PC there, so I can only suppose that there is a contact point back at the main gate. Since arriving back home I have endeavoured to find a website/email contact, but so far have been unsuccessful. Shame, I quite fancy being in email contact with a Maasai village. So, once again I met with traditional/native healers and we were able to recognise, acknowledge and understand each other – fantastic! I travelled home shortly afterwards feeling weary but exhilarated and inspired. Where next I wonder?

As it happened, it turned out to be Brittany for my next encounter with a wisewoman. A few years ago I had joined the St Buryan Twinning Association. It had been going for years, and I was under the impression that Twinning Associations involved only local dignitaries and affluent people – at least that appeared to be so from the many photographs of other towns and villages in the local paper. However, it turned out that this was not the case with our village. Another misgiving I had was that seeing as my cottage only had one bedroom, I couldn't accommodate any family in return. I was assured that this wouldn't present a problem as somebody else could put up my family when it came time for them to visit Cornwall. My final concern being whether I could afford it or not was laid to rest when I realised that due to European funding and local fund raising, the eventual cost was minimal. So the way was clear for me to visit Brittany on a reasonably regular basis.

We are twinned with a small village in Brittany called Calan and the two villages are very well suited to each other. Both are working villages and a church dominates the centre with many roads leading away from it. I was very fortunate to be placed with a family who I got on with remarkably well and their house was stunningly beautiful. It is set in the countryside within a small wood and is surrounded by wildlife – an idyllic site indeed. It was on one of the twinning days out that I had my brush with a local wisewoman...

One of the ports of call was to visit a local cider brewery and so that the guides didn't have to give two talks we were given a choice to travel with French or English speaking groups. As I like to immerse myself with the local culture I chose to travel with the Bretons. We had our tour around the ancient brewery and I was outside having a smoke. I had noticed a car pull up and a woman enter for a crate of cider which she duly placed in the boot of her car. My companion for the day called to me to come over where I found said woman obviously, given her animated gestures, recounting a story to the others. Then she smiled, waved goodbye and sped off. I turned to my friend and he told me what she had said. The story was about how to keep your man close to you, and it involved a toad. I immediately thought it was about the ubiquitous story about kissing toads – but no... What she was explaining in great detail was an ancient spell concerning toadlore that only someone who had dealings with the Old Ways would have known about. I was stunned. I tried to find out who she was and where she lived to no avail, as she just turned up at the brewery every now and then and they had no contact details. So that meeting was a bit of a tease from the gods as I couldn't pursue it any further, but at least I knew that there were still magical practitioners in Brittany. Since I have an open invitation to visit my family in Calan whenever the opportunity presents itself, I am hoping that on another visit I may be able to pursue my research into indigenous wisefolk.

TABOOS AND HERESIES

Have you ever kicked over an old dead log only to recoil back, usually with a "Yuk!" of disgust at the teeming insect life underneath? I'm fascinated by this 'Attract/Repel' response, which is both automatic and natural. Most of the situations that repel us contain an element of danger, be that disease or fear of attack and invasion. It's a primitive response to the part of life that feeds on death. Some people's responses are much stronger than others and can develop into phobias. Recognising this is probably why taboos were placed around anything that was considered 'dubious' for any reason. Over the years I have often wondered why I seem to be attracted to these places and situations. Then I discovered that the word 'taboo' means not only that something is forbidden, but also something that is sacred. That put a completely different perspective on things! I realised I was searching for the sacred, as well as exploring the forbidden out of innate curiosity. This explained somewhat why I was called wilfully wicked so many times in the past. It must have seemed that I was very perverse in my approach to things, because I would always turn things on their head to see what they looked like from that angle. This has helped me in a lot of my work with clients, being able to turn the energy around from a negative response to something more constructive. I'm the same with 'shoulds', 'musts' and 'have tos' - too dictatorial for my liking, so I turn them into 'could', 'might' and 'maybe'. Changing 'can't' into 'won't' is a real eye-opener for many, as it's more empowering.

Another example of me turning things on their head is when I looked at the other side of The Charge of the Goddess. This is a piece of inspired writing from the pen of someone who I hold in great respect, Doreen Valiente. Sadly she died a few years back, but I do have the permission of John Belham-Payne, who holds Doreen's writings, to reproduce and adapt the Charge. Here it is in its full glory:

The Charge of the Goddess

Listen to the words of the Great Mother who was of old called amongst men, Blodeuwedd, Arianrod and Cerridwen and by many other names.

"Whenever ye have need of me once in a month and better it be when the moon is full, then assemble in some secret place and adore the spirit of me who am Queen of all Witches. There shall ye meet, ye who am fain to learn all sorcery yet have not won its deepest secrets - to thee I will teach things yet unknown. And ye shall be free from all slavery and as a sign ye are truly free ye shall be naked in thine rites. And ye shall dance, sing, feast, make music and love all in mine praise - for mine is the ecstasy of the spirit and mine is also joy on earth. For my law is love unto all beings. Keep pure thine highest minds and let naught stop thee or turn thee aside, for mine is the secret door that opens onto the door of youth, and mine is the cup of wine of life and the Cauldron of Cerridwen, that is the Holy Grail of Immortality. I am the gracious Goddess who gives the gifts of joy unto the hearts of men. Upon earth I give the knowledge of the spirit eternal and then beyond death I give peace and freedom and reunion with those who have gone before. Nor do I demand sacrifice for behold I am the Mother of all living and my love is poured out upon the earth."

Hear ye the words of the Star Goddess, she in the dust of whose feet am the hosts of heaven whose body encircles the universe.

"I am the beauty of the green earth and the white moon amongst the stars and the mystery of the waters and the desire of the heart of man. Call unto thy soul arise and come unto me for I am the soul of nature who gives life everlasting to the universe. From me all things come and unto me all things must return. And before my face beloved of the gods and of men, let thine innermost divine self be enfolded in the rapture of the infinite. Let mine worship be within the heart that rejoiceth, for behold all acts of love and pleasure are my rituals. Therefore let there be strength, beauty, power and compassion, honour and humility, mirth and reverence within thee. And thou who thinkest to seek for me, know thy seeking and yearning shall avail ye nought, unless thou knowest the mystery; that if that which thou seekest, thou findest not within thee, thou wilt never find it without thee. For behold, I have been with thee at the beginning and I am that which is found at the end of desire."

This is my revised/reversed version:

The Charge of the Dark Goddess

"Listen to the words of the Dark Mother who was of old called amongst men, Hecate, Medusa, Morrigan, Erishkigal, Kali and by many other names.

Whenever you have need of me, once in a month and better it be when the moon is dark, then you shall assemble in some secret place and adore the spirit of me who is Queen of all Witches. There shall you meet, you who are fain to learn all sorcery, yet have not won its deepest secrets - to you I will teach things yet unknown. And as a sign you are truly free you shall be exposed in your rites. And you shall dance, sing, feast, make music and love all in my praise. For mine is the ecstasy of the spirit and mine is challenge upon earth - for my law is respect unto all beings. Feel deep your holy ideal, strive ever towards it and let naught persuade you nor turn you aside. For mine is the secret door that opens unto the Great Below and mine is the bitter cup of the wine of death from the Cauldron of Cerridwen which is the Black Hole of Immortality.

I am the predatory Goddess who gives the gift of fear unto the heart of man. Upon earth I give knowledge of Forbidden Arts eternal and beyond death I give peace and freedom and reunion with those who have gone before. But I do demand sacrifice for behold I am the Mother of all dead and my power is poured out upon the earth.

I am the desolation of the green earth and the dark moon amongst the stars, and the mystery of the deep, and the devourer of the hearts of men. Call unto your soul, descend and come unto me, for I am the destroyer of nature who gives rebirth to the universe. From me all things come and unto me all things must return. And before my face, feared by gods and men, let your innermost divine self be encaptured in the terror of the infinite. Let my worship be within the heart that surrenders, for behold, all acts of erotic love and lust are my rituals. Therefore let there be terrifying beauty and awesome strength, power and abandonment, honour and humility, mirth and reverence within thee. And you who think to seek for me beware, for if that which you seek you discover not within you, you will never achieve it without. For behold, I have stalked you from the beginning and I am that which is attained at the climax of desire."

I realise that in some people's minds that my rendition of the Charge could be bordering on heresy - another word with an interesting root meaning 'to choose'. Just imagine... being tortured and burnt at the stake, just for making a choice against the 'norm'. Sadly, this is what happens within a society with a 'fundamental' approach. It does not celebrate diversity – it persecutes and de-humanises through fear. Neither is this confined to the apocalyptic and superstitious mindset of medieval times. We only have to look at the last century to see what a monster can be created by everyone being the same and not stepping out of line. Hitler started with the philosophers and freethinkers (mercifully some escaped), and then moved on to anyone who was different. Disabled, mentally ill, communists, gypsies and travellers, homosexuals, Jews – you name the Scapegoat and it will be exterminated. Or ethnic cleansing as it is clinically referred to nowadays... or what I call the Tyranny of the Norm.

Cassandra's on her Soapbox.... It's true – it is something I feel passionate about. This is why I work so much on the principle of exploring and discovering all sorts of options with my clients. Some of these options will never be chosen, but just the recognition of them can empower people to change. Otherwise many clients can feel hemmed in and devoid of options, which is where the phrase 'I can't' originates. 'I won't' or 'I choose not too' are statements that come from people who are more integrated.

So here I am. Not a Hereditary Witch but a Heretical Witch! Well, that makes sense, as I have a strong belief that the Old Craft was, and remains so in some quarters, anti-establishment and subversive. This is why it's so difficult to describe Paganism as a belief system. There is no one-way of doing anything. There is no centralisation. There are organisations that endeavour to defend Pagan belief and to act as a networking system. (See Appendices for Useful Addresses.) However, these organisations are also notorious for heated debate and insurrection.

Dare I say it, but there are such people as Fundamental Pagans. They do subscribe to all the trappings of rigid religiosity – which just shows that you get dogma in all walks of life! In my opinion, don't blame the religion, rather look to the fanatics. They are the ones who spread fear, rumour and strife – and seem to get a real 'buzz' out of it. Someone once said, "Evil flourishes when good men do nothing." Having spent the majority of my younger life living in fear, I have no wish to do that for the rest of it. At the risk of sounding like Shirley Bassey, "I am what I am, and what I am needs no excuses." To me, what I do, live and believe in, makes so much sense that it feels ordinary to me. I have found that this ordinary approach makes for excellent communication with other belief systems. I don't see myself as some sort of freak or weirdo, or having supernatural powers. I am an average human being that deserves the same rights as everyone else in a so-called free country.

One thing we do have an abundance of down here in West Penwith are ancient monuments and sacred sites. There are approximately 2,000 such places on the peninsular which is an extraordinary concentration of megalithic structures. These have been in place for thousands of years, but it is only recently that these sites have come under threat, not so much from deliberate vandalism but more from the attentions of New Age tourism. Due to the rise of alternative beliefs and spiritualities, these ancient monuments have been inundated with well meaning but adverse accumulations of 'offerings'. Now I have no problem with people wanting to visit these places, but unfortunately they also feel the need to leave their mark with such things as flowers, shells, feathers, bits of rag, fruit, seeds and such like. Also fires have been lit near and sometimes on these ancient stones, destroying archaeological areas, and sometimes cracking the stones. Coins have been shoved into nooks and crannies leading to further damage because they act as wedges, and there does seem to be this urge to climb the stones whenever possible. This doesn't sound too bad until you realise that many lichens are destroyed in this way. Big deal, I hear you say, but consider – it takes roughly 15 years for lichen to grow one centimetre in length, so they're very old and slow growing and it's a shame to see the state of some of our sacred sites after a group of New Age tourists have visited. I was taught to leave nothing but your footprints and take away nothing but litter, which I feel is still relevant nowadays.

Various groups have been created to help monitor and manage these sites, and I am a Trustee and founder member of CASPN (Cornish Ancient Sites Protection Network) which is local to Penwith – see Appendix for more details. No-one wants to see the sites preserved in aspic, they are there to be utilised but common sense needs to prevail otherwise our heritage will be irreversibly damaged.

Another phenomenon I have observed in many books written by New Agers on sacred sites is the propensity to encourage people to visit these places in order to dump emotional energies. This is treating these special places as if they are psychic landfill sites, and in my book that's profanity.

If you are planning to visit our ancient sites in Cornwall please treat them with respect;

"Don't change the site – let the site change you"
(ASLAN Charter)

One of my favourite ancient sites locally is Boscawen-un stone circle and there are a few tales to tell about it...

It was a clear, still night. It was Full Moon within the haunted precincts of Boscawen-un stone circle in Cornwall. The time was many years ago when I still had the excited flush of keen exploration into the many worlds of magic. It was also a time before the hoards of ravening visitors had rediscovered our many ancient sites. Things were much quieter then. I had lit a small fire. Yes, I think a lot of people, in ignorance, did this in earlier days. However, I made sure that it was lit where others had been before and it was contained safely. The situation has now changed and I would not do this nowadays. I'm just setting the scene.

So we have lights, stage and script – all we need are the players!

It felt appropriate to call up the Horned One. I decided to really give it some 'welly' and set to with a passion. I became aware of a rustling noise coming from the eastern point of the circle, which I was facing. Then, to my absolute horror I saw a huge dark head appear with horns! I felt my hair stand on end and my eyes bulge, and then I heard... Mooooo! Yes, you guessed it. It was a curious cow, which had mooched over from the next field to see what I was doing!

I exploded into relieved laughter, and I had the distinct impression that there was an awful lot of tittering going on in the undergrowth. A classic case of getting what you ask for. Be warned. The genius loci of Boscawen-un have a very wicked sense of humour.

Boscawen-un stone circle is an exceptional place located about a mile away across the fields from where I live. It's an ancient circle consisting of nineteen stones with a large standing stone in the centre, called the King Stone. Directly opposite this in the West, is a magnificent quartz stone, locally called the Mother stone. I regularly hold Handfastings at this circle between these powerful monoliths. Boscawen-un features in many local strange tales, but I will content myself just talking about the ones that I know about personally.

Several years ago, some bright spark thought it was a good idea to light a fire on top of the King stone, which blackened it, but fortunately did not crack it. The Penwith Moot decided to take action by deciding to meet at Boscawen-un on a certain day, in order to perform an earth ritual. When we met, the rain was persisting down but a dozen brave souls had turned up. Before we entered the circle I gave a short resume of why we were there for the benefit of those who weren't at the Moot. It's useful to run through why you're there before starting any ritual. Not just to remind people of what's going on, but also it's a good way of focusing the energy. Anyway, I got to the point in my spiel where I was talking about how powerful the energies of Boscawen-un are, and was pointing my finger towards the circle... when there was a loud rumble, bang on cue! We all laughed at this synchronicity, thinking it was Concorde passing over (we often get the sonic boom over this end of Cornwall). Buoyed up by this apparent 'thumbs up' from the gods, we then went on to perform a very effective earth ritual.

The very next morning Cornwall experienced it's most powerful earthquake whose epicentre was at – yes, you guessed it - Boscawen-un! So we reckoned that what we felt the previous day was a pre-quake earth tremor. The local paper interviewed me about this, and I suggested that it was a warning growl from Mother Earth in response to desecration. Some wag wrote a letter in response saying that maybe the Penwith Moot should be liable for all the damage caused by the earthquake. Our reply was that it was An Act of God/ Goddess!

Although it was many years ago, my initiation date of August 11th was to prove important. This revealed itself later as we approached 1999. There was to be a Total Eclipse of the Sun, which could only be viewed from one place in the British Isles – West Cornwall, and the date this was to happen was August 11th. Now every year on this date I had been visiting Boscawen-un for a dedication rite, each year fortunately having the circle to myself. Things were certainly different that particular year!

There was intense media hype as the date approached and I, along with many others, was interviewed by the

162

world's media. There was much discussion concerning the weather, as Cornwall is infamous for sudden sea mists and unpredictable meteorological phenomena. This is why the Weather Forecasters always stand in front of Cornwall when they show the weather map – they really haven't a clue! Fortunately, us locals have learnt to read the signs and are generally prepared for what comes at us over the Atlantic Ocean. I was asked to perform spells for good clear weather, but made it clear that I wasn't convinced that the eclipse would be visible for the following reason:

For a lot of people the Sun and the Moon represents the God and Goddess respectively. A Total Eclipse is symbolic of the mating between them. Given that, I certainly wouldn't be surprised if They chose to draw a veil over the proceedings. After all, this is considered to be a private and sacred act and not to be looked upon.

My instincts were proved correct and there was cloud cover during the whole eclipse. However, this wasn't as disappointing as it sounds. As we weren't distracted by the, albeit beautiful, phenomenon that was happening in the heavens, we became far more sensitive to the other marvels that accompany an eclipse.

Let me set the scene for you...

Firstly a bit of background. In our CASPN meetings we were concerned with the sheer volume of people who were likely to inundate West Cornwall, and the ancient sites in particular were seen as being at risk. Our practical preparations included attracting the inevitable media interest towards certain sacred sites where Pagans were to conduct various public rituals.

This would have the result of keeping the media contained at certain places, which would subsequently protect the other more vulnerable sites. Our magical input came in the form of a press release, which I wrote with a former colleague. This not only went to the newspapers, but also appeared in all the main Pagan publications:

A Press Release on behalf of the Genius Loci of West Penwith

"Imagine if you will...living in a land where the very ground resonates with the Old Energies, where every tree, rock and stream holds its own special powers; watching and caring for the old celebration places, holy wells and healing stones; communicating with each genius loci, learning their ways, quietly and constantly.

Imagine then observing the gradual but relentless upsurge of interest in the Old Places in a New Way. This is fine but eventually the need arises for networks and organisations to protect the ancient sites from too much attention.

This is what it has been like living in West Penwith in Cornwall over the years. Now we are informed that the World and his Wife will be visiting our land next year in order to experience the total eclipse of the sun. Well, how would you feel? Guests are always very welcome but invasions are certainly not.

Local pagans, who care lovingly for the sites all year round, have decided that the best way to minimise the possibility of any damage to the sites is to hold celebrations in order to focus the energy appropriately. For this reason we are working to co-ordinate eclipse celebrations at the major ancient sacred sites in West Penwith. These open rituals will also be a way of protecting these special places from the over-enthusiastic, under educated and ignorant visitor who may be thinking of altering them. This decision has the full support of the local landowners, Penwith District Council, Cornwall Archaeology Unit and English Heritage. We have chosen Boscawen-un stone circle as the main focus of our own attention using it to link energies to all the sites. We have used this principle before to good effect; in fact the last time there was an earthquake the next morning! We invite anyone wanting to carry out a ritual at any of the major ancient sacred sites to co-operate with us in making sure that everyone gets the chance to have a meaningful spiritual experience...

We realise that the land belongs to no one and that no one can claim rights over it, however we do appeal to peoples' sense of courtesy and respect for the sacredness of the land and for the genius loci at these places. We can't be held responsible for the consequences to anyone who crassly blunders into sacred places with the intent of taking over in order to become part of a media circus. Which brings us neatly to the subject of Spriggans.

The word comes from the Cornish 'sperysyan' meaning spirits and is pronounced spridjan. People say that geese make good watchdogs. They obviously haven't met an angry Spriggan. These creatures are part of the family of Fair Folk, but are not renowned for their fair aspect. They can be particularly vicious and live only in Penwith in West Cornwall, for which the rest of Britain should be very relieved. Spriggans haunt all the ancient places, the weird and wonderful cairns, the hilltop castles, the stone circles, quoits and standing stones, and what they hate more than anything, and will attack without quarter, are those who are miserly, mean spirited and who threaten their homes.

So, who will Cornish Pagans turn to ensure that all our best-loved ancient sacred sites survive the inundation of people coming to see the eclipse next summer? Too right - we intend to get all the help we can. Starting this Samhain we will be working rituals to wake up - slowly, gently and very carefully these wild elemental spirits in which Cornwall abounds. The first ritual will aim to release and call upon these elementals from the Otherworld, which is so close and intense in Penwith. The rituals will continue each full moon up to the time of the eclipse.

We intend Britain to have a magically throbbing big toe by August next year. If the European Community were up for it, we'd also be applying for Magical Objective One Status to get our fair share of European Magical subsidy. Since the EC hasn't got this sorted out yet, we would welcome appropriate magical assistance from anyone who would like to 'link in' to our efforts. We look forward to interesting energy surges in our full moon rituals from Samhain onwards. It goes without saying, that we will be thanking and returning the spirits to their former state after the eclipse.

Warning

Be afraid - be very afraid - if you have any ideas of being disrespectful to any of our ancient sites next August. There is an old Cornish saying; 'there isn't a hedge without an ear, or a down without an eye!' In normal times you are likely to be seen or heard if you get up to no good. Next year you may get set upon by Spriggans who are known for their wicked sense of humour and timing, and don't count on Spriggans understanding the concept of a proportionate response. If you do decide to visit their abodes you are advised to add nothing nor take anything away. Spriggans like their homes just the way they are and don't take too kindly to anyone doing a spot of interior decorating without permission!

Of course we, and the Spriggans, will welcome anyone who comes with respect for our ancient sacred landscape and treats it and all the residents, both material and otherworldly, with courtesy. We leave the rest to your imagination."

This met with a mixed response, but at least thankfully there was no reported damage to sites following the eclipse.

On the day itself a small group of us, including a high profile American wizard called Oberon Zell, set off from my cottage to walk across the fields to Boscawen-un. Our aim was to facilitate the ritual and liaise with the media, which had gathered in force and was waiting for our arrival at the circle. Once there, we laid down a few ground rules including keeping the film crews out of the circle and to avoid flash photography during the eclipse. One East European film crew decided to flout these guidelines immediately and entered the circle. It was heartening to see all the other film crews turning on them and threatening to block their shots if they continued in their aggressive behaviour. The offending crew decided to leave and the rest of us prepared for the unique experience to come.

As I suspected the skies remained overcast, but what we did witness was remarkable. The first thing that was noted was the moon's shadow, which seemed to clump it's way across the clouds; a sudden breeze sprang up and all birdsong ceased. There was complete silence with none of the sounds usually associated with the countryside like cattle lowing. Gradually we became aware that there was a 360-degree sunset around us. It was an awesome sight. I can quite understand the primitive minds of our ancestors thinking that the world was coming to an end. It looked very primeval, much like you would imagine the beginnings of time.

I personally found it a very moving and emotional experience, and judging by the looks on everyone's faces afterwards, so did many others. There was almost a party spirit prevailing following the eclipse with food and drink shared amongst us all. We were interviewed live by many film crews from around the world and watched many of them later on television when we returned home. I was glad that we had insisted on silence during the eclipse as we saw that many gatherings of people celebrated the experience in a different way, accompanied by much cheering and a myriad of flashing lights from all the cameras. It appeared that everyone had a great time and a sense of optimism and euphoria abounded for the rest of the day. It was an unforgettable experience and I can relate very much to why some people become eclipse-chasers!

Apart from working with CASPN mentioned previously, my voluntary work includes working for the Pagan Federation. This is an organisation, set up over 35 years ago, that focuses on anti-defamation, networking and campaigns for religious recognition. At the time of writing I am on the Pagan Federation Committee as the Community Services Officer, which covers Prison Visiting, Hospital Visiting and Interfaith. The last thing I thought I would be doing is sitting on any sort of committee but here I am about to take on the role of Vice President, which will cover campaigning. Interestingly after the 2001 census, Paganism was calculated to be the 7th largest religion in the British Isles. This was an important breakthrough as the Home Office has been communicating with us regarding education, hospitals, prisons and the like since. All this activism is crucial to help re-educate the general public about Paganism in general and witchcraft in particular. The quality of people's lives depends on this, as prejudice and ignorance can cause untold harm as seen in the 'Satanic Ritual Abuse' scandal that happened back in the late eighties.

Basically, this was a modern day witch-hunt, which originated in the Bible Belt in America and spread to the UK through scare mongering via our Social Services. Self appointed 'experts' who were heavily influenced by a fundamentalist Christian attitude appeared on chat shows and delivered seminars about a 'Satanic Ritual Abuse' conspiracy supposedly running rampant through our communities. The social services establishment unfortunately took these diatribes seriously, resulting in traumatic dawn raids on many households where their children were forcibly taken into care and interrogated. Rochdale, Cleveland and Orkney were high profile examples of this and hysteria in the form of a moral panic gripped society. This is exactly the same energy that was responsible for witchcraft persecutions centuries before, and Pagan parents lived in fear of that knock on the door. Eventually Professor La Fontaine was commissioned to write a government report about the phenomenon; this declared that there was no factual evidence to support any of these allegations.

The notion of a baby-killing and orgiastic Devil-worshipping conspiracy is a complete fantasy, but one that has throughout history been used to sanction the most brutal and inhuman pogroms – notably by Rome against the first Christians, then by Christians against Jews, heretics and witches, and so on. It is a variant of ethnic cleansing based on religious fanaticism.

This is why education and information regarding Paganism is so crucial. At present in the Pagan Federation we are compiling factual information for the benefit of Social Services so that these appalling miscarriages of justice can be avoided.

Some say that politics and religion don't mix and should be kept apart. I disagree with this. As far as I'm concerned it's impossible to separate the two if your beliefs embrace any sense of community. Politics is about people, and people matter. Community matters if we are ever going to live in any sort of harmony with others and the creatures that populate our planet.

One of the best ways to keep a sense of community alive and well is through festivals and celebrations. I am much heartened by the revival of many rural feasts and festivities locally and nationally. Many villages and towns throughout Cornwall still celebrate their individual Feast Days – in St Buryan it falls on the weekend nearest to May 13th (Old Beltane). Old customs still survive such as Padstow 'Obby 'Oss and Helston Flora and The Old Cornwall Society keep alive old traditions like Crying the Neck, and the Summer Solstice beacon fires. It's truly inspiring to be on top of Chapel Carn Brea (First & Last hill) when the first fire is lit on St John's Eve and to turn around and watch, weather permitting, the next beacon spring into life – and then the next and so on right up the spine of Cornwall.

The weekend following this is the Mazey Day celebrations. Mazey is a Cornish term for crazy, maddened or intoxicated and is therefore very appropriate for this lively festival! It is a Midsummer festival revived in 1991 which epitomises a true community celebration. I was unable to attend the very first festival but have played an active part since then. It's the one time of the year when I perform weather magic so that the processions are seen at their best. I exert a considerable amount of energy into this and no parade has been rained upon since I started. However, I have been quite peeved when each year the Mayor takes credit for the fine weather!

The weekend kicks off with Mazey Eve, which keeps alive the spirit of anarchy by having the Mock Mayor elections. Anyone may stand for election and the more crazy the manifesto the better. My particular favourite was the year Penzance elected a Jack Russell terrier called Buster - although I also had a fondness for Helgar the Hormonal who promised every woman in Penzance their own individual fireman! A magnificent firework display follows this and then it's time to gather around a certain stable door down by the harbour for the annual appearance of our very own 'Obby 'Oss – Penglaz!

Penglaz is an extraordinary folklore figure that both scares and amazes the young and old alike. She is what is known as a 'skull and pole' or mast horse and is well over seven foot tall in height. With fiercely snapping jaws she dances and lunges her way through the crowded streets accompanied by a Teazer (Yours Truly) who also has a snapper as a baton.

Penglaz is the Penzance 'Obby 'Oss first described in the 19th century following mummers, dancers and guisers at high holidays and feast days

The modern Penglaz, revived in 1992, appears late at night, true to form as a Nightmare, to beguile and frighten the Golowan revellers. Based on the description of Penglaz by Penzance antiquarians the 'Obby 'Oss is surrounded by secrecy and myth and is now a tradition jealously guarded by Penzance folk.

Penglaz also visits the recently revived Montol Midwinter festival thereby confirming her status as a Solstice 'Oss governing Death/Rebirth.

The Teazer is also known locally as the Bucca. Dependant on the time of year, this character appears as Bucca Gwidden (White - Midsummer) or Bucca Dhu (Black - Midwinter)

Over the years Penglaz has become an iconic feature of the Solstice Festivals, however no one knows when or where she will appear lurching, dancing and snapping out of the darkness. Penglaz is a wild, anarchic figure and cannot be tamed, and was once described as 'the most frightening folklore image'.

The wild music is provided by The Golowan Band which is our very own 'ambling, rambling' band made up of about thirty-odd local musicians. I love their music and it was only recently when they brought out their first CD that I realised how very talented they all are. I defy anyone who hears their tunes not to want to get up and dance to them.

Teazing Penglaz is highly energetic as it's part of my role to make space for her to move through the crowds, so there's precious little time to actually dance - I'm too busy shoving people out of the way. When Penglaz appears the crowd are also dancing the Serpent Dance, which winds its way up and down and round the streets, so you can see I've got my work cut out! This is one of the reasons why I dance with the

Band in the processions on Mazey Day – no pushing and shoving there. The other reason is that I use the energy of the dance to conjure up the weather magic. In the last couple of years I have started to take a band of Merry Mazey Maids to dance with me. They are youngsters from my own village – one of whom is a vicar's daughter! They are very good and the onlookers love to see them perform.

People often ask me where I get my energy from over the weekend as my dancing and teazing is far from decorous and involves leaps and high kicks. I answer that it just kind off takes me over... although recently I have begun to suffer from injuries afterwards and am sometimes seen the week following Mazey sporting a walking stick. I am in the process of searching for an appropriate person(s) that I can train up to eventually take over my performance roles, but I hope to be able to continue for a few more years yet. At the very least until I become a pensioner.

Unlike many, I'm quite looking forward to reaching retirement age. Just imagine, being paid a sum of money each week for managing to stay on the planet that long! I really thought that I would die young and not make old bones, but I'm still here and although I will reach retirement age soon, I doubt whether my work as a wisewoman will grind to a halt. I'll slow down no doubt and see less clients but hopefully be able to give more talks. I'll probably die in harness.

Since I wrote this, many things have come to pass. Due to the retirement of the Old 'Oss and rider, a new 'Oss needed to be crafted and this was successfully achieved in 2008. The Penglaz Co-operative was formed which raised money by selling Penglaz memorabilia (Tee shirts, card, prints etc) in order to create a new Penglaz. She is a skilfully engineered 'Oss that is very versatile in movement and will probably outlive us all. Also we now have a team of robust, fit riders and a very talented second Teazer who is ready to take over at any point should the need arise. In the meantime we both work in synchronicity to teaze Penglaz through the streets of Penzance. Now I can rest assured that the Penglaz tradition will survive and continue for future generations to enjoy.

Or maybe not....! Just when I thought I could relax and start to enjoy my retirement, a series of events occurred in 2010 which culminated in the Old 'Oss coming back and ousting what was set up to replace her. Time to move on methinks. We still have a wonderful 'Oss and team so a change of image and name is required. There's life in the Old Girl yet!

Just before we go to print I am delighted to announce the rebirth of our 'Oss and team. The result following an intriguing make-over is Boekka & Penkevyll the Lands End Oss.

Here's an excerpt from our website:

"The original idea of bringing together Border Morris with an 'Obby 'Oss was first created on 8th August 2010 and we use this date as an anniversary for our side.

Penkevyll the 'Oss had a former existence as a replacement Penglaz (Penzance 'Oss) when the original revived Penglaz retired in April 2008. Sadly due to ongoing internal wranglings with another rival replica Penglaz, the original Penglaz felt the need to make a comeback thereby ousting both replacement 'Osses.

We, as in an 'Oss and 2 Teazers, withdrew and gave our 'Oss a makeover plus a new name

– Penkevyll (Cornish for horse's head). We had
already begun to perform dance routines with our
'Oss so we simply changed our kit colours and our
side name to Boekka (Cornish for scarecrow).

None of this happened overnight – we stripped
the 'Oss of its coloured tatters and back to its basic
covering of black material (We were loath to part
with this as it had been quite expensive in terms
of quantity of fire retardant cloth). We wanted the
'Oss to have ears and so a pair of leather ones were
lovingly crafted and, all in all, the overall look we
were left with was spooky and gothic! We decided
to introduce the occasional colours of midnight
blue and dark, blood red to the black which made
the Teazers resemble undertakers when attired
in their tailcoats and top hats. The Guisers
worked within the same colour spectrum but with
midnight blue shirts and tattered waistcoats plus
beribboned top hats. The Teazers are distinctive in
that they carry snappers with which to 'teaze' the
'Oss and occasionally the unsuspecting onlookers!

One of the criticisms aimed at us whilst working
with Penglaz was that we were too Pagan; but
now as an independent side we feel free to express
that wild, anarchic part that seemed to disturb
and unnerve some members within certain local
festival committees.

With that in mind, we are actively recruiting
for dark, edgy folk to be dancers (Guisers) and
musicians who are also dedicated, committed and
not afraid of hard work. We will be travelling to 2
- 3 festivals and conferences/gatherings each year
as well as appearances at local venues around the
Land's End Peninsula. Please contact us if you are
interested in joining our eldritch tribe..."

To find out more contact our website (see Useful Resources).

THE LORE OF THE LAND

One of the most crucial aspects of being a wisewoman is her relationship with the community and the Land. By Land I'm not just talking about Britain or even the world, although that visionary aspect is relevant. In my particular case I am referring to the Land where I live, the West Cornwall peninsular. To myself and many others, it is a magical landscape. Its main geological make up is granite, and there are many structures both old and new which incorporate this local stone. When I wander across the moors and fields I come across many outcrops of granite, which to me represent the 'bones of the land' and its ancientness lies very close to the surface. Others may call the land down here bleak; I see it as wild and rugged.

After dark, West Cornwall becomes a liminal land, a sort of cross between Deliverance and Brigadoon, especially when the mists descend or on a moonlit night. Every now and then I go for a moonlight walk which opens up my Deep Mind, a magical seeing that takes me back to my childhood. These jaunts are very helpful in learning to listen to the Land. Even simply sitting in my garden teaches me about the Drama of Life.

We can spend so much time whizzing around, or even

if sat still our minds are still preoccupied with things we have to do. Very little time is put aside to just 'being in the moment' and experiencing the 'now'. I often advise my clients to utilise what I call Mars Magic – Work – Rest – and Play. Mostly we are good at Work and Play but Rest is often forgotten and overlooked as something that we don't have time for. So we end up living our lives at breakneck speed and never find time to just 'be'. The Druids had a concept called Walking with Grace. Now this has nothing to do with being elegant, this is moving through space with total awareness of everything we are doing. Some oriental disciplines call this concept, Mindfulness. Try it sometime with doing something very ordinary like washing up. Lots of people find this an onerous task, but when you think about it, it's actually very pleasant. Your hands are immersed in warm, soapy water; the outcome is an array of clean, sparkling crockery and cutlery; and if you are fortunate enough, like me, to have a beautiful panorama to gaze upon out of your window, the whole process can be wonderfully satisfying and restful. This simple way of existing can remove the stresses and strains of 21st Century life, where most people are thinking about 10 steps ahead of whatever it is that they are doing, thereby missing out on the simple contentment of the work at hand.

The Cornish, being a traditionally mystic people were, and still are to a large extent, close to the world of the fairy folk. One only has to read the old tales of the droll tellers to realise that the Fair Folk were classed under three main types: Spriggans, Knockers and Piskys.

Spriggans, already referred to earlier in this book, are

darker spirits that haunt wild and lonely places such as old ruins, barrow mounds, quoits and other megalithic monuments. Their function is to be guardians of treasure, and as such are renowned for dispensing summary justice to those who fail to show appropriate respect to the ancient sites.

Knockers are basically mine spirits, although there have been references made to them frequenting wells. These subterranean entities were much respected and honoured by the Cornish miners who often left offerings of tallow and pieces of pasty in order to appease them. In return the Knockers would alert the miners by knocking sounds when a collapse was imminent, or direct the miners to rich lodes. Whistling, spying on their activities or making the sign of the cross offended them. Belief in Knockers has declined along with the mining industry in Cornwall, although they are still thought to exist in the old mine workings, wells and deep caves.

Finally Piskys are generally perceived to be cheerful pranksters who delight in leading people astray. Practically everyone I know, including myself has been pisky-led. What this means in practical terms is; you are travelling towards a place where you have been many times and no matter what you do, you can't find it. It can be most frustrating if you don't recognise what is happening. There is an antidote: the way to stop this mischievous enchantment is to stop and turn your coat or jacket inside out. That may sound odd, but I can assure you that it works.

One aspect unites all these fair folk: they abhor meanness of spirit and any form of miserliness. However, they respond positively to creativeness, music, erotica and generosity. Admirable traits in my opinion!

Also within the Cornish drolls are tales of local characters who were wisefolk. A local folklorist for research purposes counted up how many wisefolk operated in Devon and Cornwall at the turn of the last century – it was over sixty. Given the population at the time, that was a high incidence. I will make reference to a few who are local to my area.

I will start with my favourite, Old Granny Boswell. As her name suggests, she was Romany and was married to Ephraim Boswell who was also known as King of the Gypsies. Following the death of her husband, Granny Boswell's main stamping ground was Helston – and in particular the Blue Anchor public house; she was very fond of the local ale, Spingo! She was known for being outspoken, often the worse for wear following long sessions in the Blue Anchor, thereby becoming a public nuisance, and bizarre in dress; even nowadays a local saying is: 'All dressed up like Granny Boswell!'

However, none of the above stopped her from being a formidably powerful wisewoman and her magical capabilities were intact in spite of the Spingo – perhaps because of it! In honour of Granny Boswell I have just raised a glass of Spingo to her as I write this. I usually go out and spend some time at her graveside, which is local, and take a bottle with me. I find this to be a very effective way of communicating with the ancestors, or in this case, craft predecessors. Every now and then when I've got a thorny craft problem to work through, I go and talk it over with her – imagine what she would have done and adapt it for use.

Her most famous or infamous public example of her

powers happened in Coinagehall St, Helston, the year was 1906...

It was Election Day and the Tory Party caused a sensation by using a brand new automobile, the first seen in Helston, to ferry voters to and from the Polling Station. Said vehicle was about to pull out on another journey when Granny Boswell came reeling drunk out the Blue Anchor and stood swaying in front of the gleaming, pounding motor. Unfortunately the driver simply yelled rudely to her to clear off out of the way. This did not sit well with the inebriated Granny Boswell and she let forth a stream of invective accompanied by some very salty swearing. This ended with her delivering the pronouncement that the automobile would not reach the end of the street. Sure enough the machine came to an abrupt halt with a loud bang halfway down Coinagehall Street – one of it's tension rods had broken and the automobile had to be towed away by a horse. Granny Boswell's street cred shot up as she was seen to have successfully placed a curse on an automobile!

Which just goes to show that within the tradition of cunning women, there is a lot of subversive wildness in their characters. I do have these qualities quietly simmering (most of the time) inside me but I need to adapt to the 21st Century and find different uses for these passions.

I could go on about the many pellars and cunning folk in Cornwall like Madgy Figgy, Tammy Blee etc but there are some very good books written in depth about the subject, so I'll leave it there for now.

CUNNING LORE

The final part of this book will be dedicated to Cornish Cunning Lore and contains various spells, charms and rituals. They are not meant to be a recipe book to be followed slavishly; they are included as an example of the ingenuity required to effectively work with the spirit world and local environment. They are included as items of interesting folk magic and anyone wanting to replicate any of these practices takes full personal responsibility for the outcome.

With thanks to Cecil Williamson for his extensive research into the practices of the Wayside Witch.

CHARMS

Apple, Potato and Pins Charm
Breaking spell:
Stick pins into an apple or potato and hang it up. Leave to dry and shrivel.
Making spell:
Bury same and perform bonfire ritual over the spot.

Charm Water
Gather nine quartz stones from a running stream taking care not to disturb the free flow of water. Collect water – do not dip against the flow. Make the stones red-hot and drop into the water. Bottle and use whenever necessary.

Arrow Head Flint

It is believed that these flints impart virtue to water in which they have been soaked, and that diseases have been cured by drinking it.

Safety Charm

Pluck ten blades of yarrow – keep nine – cast the tenth away as tithe for the spirits. Put the nine in your stocking under the heel of the right foot – when going on a journey and then no harm can come to you.

Knotted String Charm

Touch the trouble or symbol of same; or if warts touch them with a knot. (There should be as many knots as are warts) Then bury it. The best place is near the sea at the low water mark. Turn, walk away – do not turn around or retrace your steps for 24 hours. As the charm decays so the trouble fades away.

Adder Charm

The slough of an adder hung on the rafters preserves the house against fire.

Protection Charm Bag

Within a bag made of red flannel:
A pinch of salt in a twist of red paper
Seven peppercorns in a twist of blue paper
A pinch of oak wood ash in a twist of white paper
A rabbit's foot
A cock's spur
A red rose bud

A white rosebud

Lumbago Charm

Take three green stones gathered from a running brook, between midnight and morning, while no word is said. In silence it must be done. Then uncover the limb and rub each stone several times closely downwards from hip to the toe saying:

> "Wear away, wear away
> There you shall not stay
> Cruel pain
> Away, away"

Then rid yourself of the stones giving them to some other living thing by secret cunning.

Charm for stomach pains

> "May Peter take
> May Paul take
> May Michael take the pain away
> The cruel pain that kills the back and the life
> And darkens the eyes"

This oration is written and tied to a hare's foot and is always to be worn by the person afflicted and hung round the neck.

Hot Cross Buns

In Cornish farmhouses the Cross-bun may be seen hanging by a string to the Bacon Rack; slowly diminishing until the return of the season replaces it with a fresh one. It is of sovereign good in all manner of diseases afflicting the family and cattle. I have more than once seen a little of this cake grated into a warm mash for a sick cow.

Snails

A girl can wish illicit love from a man by inducing him to carry a snail shell, which she has had for sometime about her person.

To present a snail shell is to make a very direct but not very delicate declaration of love to anyone.

Snails are a type of voluptuousness because they are hermaphrodite and exceedingly given to sexual indulgence, so that as many as half a dozen may be found mutually giving and taking pleasure.

To know the name of the person you are destined to marry, put a snail on a plate of flour – cover it over and leave it all night; in the morning the initial letter of the name will be found traced on the flour by the snail.

Love Charm

This is a charm set for Love; a woman's charm of love and desire; a charm of god that none can break.

"You for me
And I for thee
And for none else
Your face to mine
And your head turned
Away from others"

This is to be repeated three times secretly over a drink

given to the beloved.

HERB LORE

A childless woman is considered to have the strongest power over the secrets of herbs, especially those used for maladies of children.

There are seven herbs that nothing natural or supernatural can injure:- Vervain, St John's Wort, Speedwell, Eyebright, Mallow, Yarrow and Self Help (Heal?). But they must be pulled at noon on a bright day, near the Full of the Moon to have full power.
The seven magical woods: Oak, Ash, Beech, Holly, Elm, Chestnut and Willow.

The wisewoman or green doctor never revealed the nature of the herb used and always gathered the herbs herself at night and hid them under the eaves of the house. If a person who carried the herb let it fall to the ground by the way, it lost its power; and if they talked of it or showed it to anyone, all the virtue went out of it. It was to be used secretly and alone, and then the cure would be perfected without fail.

It is said by the wisewoman and fairy doctors that the roots of the Elder tree and Apple tree that bears red apples, if boiled together and drunk fasting, will expel any evil living thing or evil spirit that may have taken up its abode in the body of a man.

The root of the Sea Poppy so much valued for removing all pains in the breast, stomach and intestines is good also for disordered lungs. It is so much better here than in other places that the apothecaries of Cornwall send hither for it; and some people plant them in their gardens in Cornwall and will not part with them under sixpence a root.

This root is accounted very good both as an emetic and a cathartic. If therefore it is designed that it shall operate as the former, then it should be scraped and sliced upwards – that is beginning from the root the knife is to ascend towards the leaf – but if it is intended to operate as a cathartic, it must be scraped downwards towards the root. The Senecio or groundsel is stripped of its leaf upwards for an emetic and downwards for a cathartic.

In Cornwall all medicinal plants are gathered when the moon is just such an age as suits the ritual as laid down. When gathering the herb called Samolus (Marshwort) or fen-berries, the wisewoman has first to fast for a day, and then not to look backwards when plucking it, and lastly only the left hand may be used. Here it is of interest to note that the word Samol in the Phoenician tongue means left hand. This herb is to be particularly efficacious in curing the diseases of pigs and cattle.

The Blue Scabious

The Blue Scabious in Cornwall is never plucked. It is called the 'Devil's Bit' and should it be picked it is held that they will haves nightmares and ill fortune.

Charm for Cattle

Branches of care (rowan) are hung over cattle stalls to prevent them being ill wishes. Slips of care were also carried in the pocket – very good against the rheumatism.

Bramble charm

Charm for curing weak eyes by twirling a piece of smouldering bramble stalk in front of his face. (Ludgvan)

Old Dartmoor Verse

"Oak Logs will warm you well,
That are old and dry.
Logs of pine will sweetly smell
But the sparks will fly.

Birch logs will burn too fast,
Chestnut scarce at all;
Hawthorn logs are good to last –
Cut them in the fall.

Holly logs will burn like wax,
You may burn them green;
Elm logs like smouldering flax,
no flame to be seen.

Beech logs for wintertime,
Yew logs as well;
Green elder logs it is a crime
For any man to sell.

Pear logs and apple logs,
They will scent your room;
Cherry logs across the dogs
Smell like flower of broom.

Ash logs, smooth and grey,
Burn them green or old,
Buy up all that come your way –
Worth their weight in gold."

The Reason Why There Is Witchcraft

To various conspicuous and easily intelligible causes the
witch and the warlock like the necromancer and the
astrologer owed their power to the multitude.

First there is the eager desire which humanity not
unnaturally feels to tear aside the veil of Death and
obtain some knowledge of 'The Otherworld', which is
hidden so completely from it.

Next must be taken into account, man's greed for
temporal advantages, his anxiety to direct the course
of events to his personal benefit; and lastly his malice
against his fellows.

Thus we see that the influence enjoyed by the Sorcerer
and the Witch had its origins in the unlawful passions
of humanity – and don't you ever forget it!

DARKER REALMS

Sticks

White thorn is a very unlucky companion on journeys.
A hazel switch brings good luck and has power over
evil.

Cornish Miners

Bulhorns (snails) when met by miners in their path
were commonly propitiated with a bit of tallow from

their candles.

Scaw

The stable door at night was fastened with a green twig of Scaw (Elder) to keep out unnatural intruders from horses

Grave Dew Charm

Before sunrise on May 1st go to a grave that contains both male and female. Cover grave with a white absorbent cloth. After paying appropriate tithe to the spirits remove cloth and squeeze collected dew into a small bowl. Decant into a bottle. To be kept and used for acts of eldritch potency.

Charms from Moths

In Cornwall, and many other parts of the world, it is believed that moths represent departed souls. As creatures of the hours of darkness they may be used in spells for harm, for help, protection, ghosts, nightmares, evil spirits, death in the dark etc.

Pay particular attention to signs and marks on the wings for many secret symbols may be found read and understood by the Adept who has been well versed in the fundamental teachings of the Art.

Ill Wishing Basket

Basket containing the following items all broken with an oblong stone: one looking glass, a small glass bottle, a cup and saucer, a small plate. Cover with earth from a female grave. On top place three lumps of white quartz and then cover with a white cloth which has a hole burnt in it. Finally break the handle of the basket.

Take basket and deposit on victim's doorstep. Each action in preparing the basket is done to the accompaniment of an elaborate spoken ritual.

This curse is unique in that it leaves a loophole of escape from harm. Reverse the spell by mending and restoring all objects and all intended harm will be thrown back on the person who compounded the charm.

To Bring Harm to a Person who has Done Someone a Grievous Harm

Prepare and make a small loaf of bread except that one mixes in enough soot to blacken the mixture. Before baking, christen the loaf in the victim's name and mark name in loaf (initials will do). While loaf is baking mark and christen a knife with the name of person wronged. Whilst pronouncing curse, plunge the knife into the heart of the baked loaf. Hang up transfixed loaf in a secret place. As the loaf mildews and rots, so the victim fails. (Camborne)

Dance with the Wind

The holy fathers of the Christian church proclaimed from the pulpit that all destructive storms and tempests were the creation of the devil and his minions, the witches.

Proof, they claimed, was evident in the fact that witches haunted the quaysides of harbours soliciting seafaring men to purchase their charms and spells against the cruel sea.

Further proof was to be found in the fact that witches frequented vantage points, set high up on the cliff tops, when high seas and storms were raging. There, in unison and harmony with the storm, they swirled and turned, shrieking and howling, into the face of the wind.

Yes, witches did sell advice about forthcoming weather conditions to seamen. Like their cat familiars they could sense and predict changes in the weather. Their predictions were consistently accurate, and seafarers considered their advice to be money well spent.

Yes, witches did, and still do, dance with the wind, in high places above the sea. You should try it sometime. It is an experience never to be forgotten. I can guarantee that you will be carried away by the wind. You will experience greater emotional release and revelation than is obtainable by the use of the most potent, and lethal, of drugs. For you have cast yourself into the arms of the universal creator.

In those fleeting moments you experience the full power and awesome majesty of our creator and benefactor.

RITUALS

Invocation to the Goddess

> "We invoke and call upon thee
> Fairer than night and silver clad
> Queen of the moonlit sea
> Of all magic and all hunting
> Earth Mother
> Flowers of the field
> Moon and all its mysteries
> Queen of Elphame reign

Come to us from afar
All hail to thee!"

Invocation of the God

"Lord of the Hunt
And King of Elphame reign
Cross thy woodland course
And meet with us again
We call upon thee
Might Faerie King
To come once more unto they Faerie Ring
Lord of Sun and Oak be here
Among thy faerie priests
Who hold thee dear."

The Rite of Calling Down the Moon

"I salute and conjure thee
O beauteous Moon
Now is the kindling time of night
When all witches shall make due sacrifice
Enchanting down
The vessel of our frame.
An breath in deep
The Goddess's sweet kiss
Invoke, invoke
They powers that ancient bide
An come to me
Who freely wait for thee
With spells and chants

VILLAGE WITCH

To call down my mistern moon
'Till She come down
An I am blessed be
O beauteous Moon
I conjure thee.

By the air which I breathe
By the breath which is within me
I conjure thee
By the earth that I touch
By the light that I breathe
By the waters of the night
I conjure thee.

Consumed in witch fire
Mine body descends
Thy fire sweet Goddess
Burns in mine mind
Candles all within the circle bound
Illumined by the moon's light silvered frame
An passage by the witch blade
For to haime
An floating in the moon's sweet sleeping arms
Thy presence breathing in
An breathing out.

An fly alone with Nature by my side
Till honeyed breath
Come blow me then about
Down, down Merry Moon
Thy ancient power bides

THE LORE OF THE LAND

Down, down the witch's boon
Thine blessings ancient Bride.

I am a child of the Moon
Reborn of shining light
In it's silvered glittering haze
I see my Goddess and myself."

Power Raising Chant

"Ancient Ones cast thy blessings
Down into thy round
Watch thy witches spin and reel
And dance upon the ground

Magic of Earth and power of stone
Clay of our flesh
Soil of our bones
Nourish the web of night and day
Spin the wheel
IO EVOHE!

Magic of thought
Power of Air
Wind that blows
Without any a care
Blow the web of night and day
Spin the wheel
IO EVOHE!

Magic of Water

Glistening free
Power of deepest emerald sea
Sprinkle the web of night and day
Spin the wheel
IO EVOHE!

Magic of Fire
Princes of flame
Whose sun riseth higher
Than any man's name
Warm the web of night and day
Spin the wheel
IO EVOHE!"

Invitation to the Fair Folk

"By the Moon Queen's mystic light
By the hush of holy night
By the woodland deep and green
By the starlight's silver sheen
By the zephyr's whispered spell
Brooding powers invisible
Faerie Court and Elven Throng
Unto whom the groves belong
And by Laws of ancient date
Found in the scrolls of Faerie Fate
Stream and fount are dedicate
Wheresoe'er your feet today
Far from haunts of men may stray
We adjure you, stay no more
Exiles on an alien shore

THE LORE OF THE LAND

But with spells of magic birth
Once again make glad the earth."

EPILOGUE

Incredibly it has taken me 10 years to get to the completion of my book. The first draft was finished several years ago, but my publishers at the time did not agree with the inclusion of the autobiographical material at the beginning. They just wanted the witchy bits, plus a sort of spell recipe book at the end. I wasn't happy with this for a couple of reasons... Firstly it was a formula that had been repeated time and again in other books over the years and I wanted my book to be different; and secondly, the one thing I was always asked time after time following talks was how I became a village wisewoman, and I wanted to tell the story of my journey. Over the years I tried to adapt to what my original publishers wanted, but it just felt like the heart had gone out of what I was writing. Thankfully, just recently I discovered that the answer was just around the corner with local publishers, Troy Books.

Given the passage of time, quite a few things that I had written years ago have moved on, or changed in some way. I considered going back and altering these extracts but realised that the book has evolved and I need to show that journey also. Some important life-changing events have happened that I definitely hadn't foreseen – but I'm wise enough to realise that I don't know everything, and I'm sometimes wrong about things. For instance, I thought it highly unlikely that at this late point in my life that I would finally meet my match and fall in love – but I did! And the bonus is that my partner has also taken on the roles of Apprentice and Teazer, so that for these traditions the future is now secure leaving me free to retire – which I did on the Spring Equinox March 21st 2010.

Finally, I feel very blessed to be able to end this book on a real high. I was Handfasted, according to the Old Ways, to my beloved Laetitia on Samhain October 31st 2010 in Boscawen-un stone circle, witnessed by many honoured guests including Penglaz, Merv the Cornish Piper and of course not forgetting the Ancestors and the Old Ones.

The circle is now complete.

Useful Resources

Books
I realise that most of the following books are over 40 years old, and I have attempted to include more modern, contemporary works. However, in all honesty I haven't come across many that I would consider recommending to others with regard to my type of magical practice. It is worth bearing in mind also, that the prohibitive price of some publications has prevented me from extending my reading list further, and I will not recommend if I haven't read a book myself.

Mastering Witchcraft
Paul Huson
Corgi

Mastering Herbalism
Paul Huson
Abacus

The Devil's Picturebook
Paul Huson
Abacus

Witchcraft for Tomorrow
Doreen Valiente
Robert Hale

The Triumph of the Moon
Ronald Hutton
Oxford

Tammy Blee's Cabalistic Agency - Witchcraft and Popular Magic in History
and Interpretation
Jason Semmens
Exeter: Privately Printed 2016

Usually recommended books are predominantly non-fiction but I am making an exception to that general rule with the inclusion of some of the works of Terry Pratchett. For years and years when he was 'all the rage' I deliberately avoided reading him as I have a perverse streak in me that avoids fads and trends. It was only after being told repeatedly over the years that I, my attitude and my practice, was reminiscent of Granny Weatherwax that I eventually succumbed and read Wyrd Sisters. I began to see their point and was suitably impressed with Terry Pratchett's unique slant on life, especially the worlds magical so I read the rest of the Witches' books. He definitely had that certain something that I call a cunning wisdom and I therefore recommend his works to you.

Although the following books fall under the category of Young Adults Fiction, there are valuable lessons to learn about the training of a young witch to be found here – as well as a lot of laughs!
The Wee Free Men
A Hat Full of Sky
Wintersmith
I Shall Wear Midnight
The Shepherd's Crown
Terry Pratchett
Doubleday

Websites
My website
www.villagewisewoman.co.uk

My blog
www.grumpyoldwitchcraft.com

Obby Oss website
www.boekka.blogspot.co.uk

A must-see museum for followers of the Old Ways
www.museumofwitchcraft.com

Book illustrations and cover design
www.celticmystery.co.uk

Book photographer
www.johnisaac.co

Local woodland burial site
www.woodlandburialplace.co.uk

Innovative and creative website that focuses on Cornwall and spirit of place
www.geniusloci.co.uk

Golowan's official website
www.golowan.org

CASPN official website
www.cornishancientsites.com

Oldest British Pagan networking/campaigning organisation
www.paganfed.org

An Addendum

I t's been about 18 months since my book was first published
and I must say that I've been very pleasantly surprised at the
reaction to it. Reviews have been positive and I have heard
from a considerable amount of people, particularly women, who
have been very moved as they could relate a lot to what I had
written. They have said that they also found it very inspiring,
which is so rewarding to hear after agonising for ages about how
much to disclose about myself. I have only received one common
'complaint' and that being that they were disappointed that there
wasn't more to read! Apparently many folks had whizzed through
the book at a rate of knots, sometimes they read it in a day, which
I find extraordinary. Well, the fact of the matter is that because it
took so long to write 'Village Witch', I had no plans for embarking
on such an endeavour ever again – but here I am prattling on
once more…!

So, all I can say is that I *may* write some memoirs when I get
time from my busy schedule. Wherever did I get the idea that
retirement would mean that life would ease down and I'd have
more time for myself? There have been major changes since I
fell in love and got Handfasted, and I soon found out that marriage
throws up its own unique challenges – especially after living for

over forty years on my own! I've often wondered why there were so many superstitions surrounding weddings and I found out soon enough… People can really change in an adverse way following an erstwhile single person marrying and we certainly found out who our true friends were…and who were not! They say that True Love never runs smooth, and that is absolutely correct! However, the sort of experiences and challenges we have had to face has tried and tested our relationship to its utmost, but fortunately it has ultimately strengthened and deepened our love for each other in ways I never dreamed of. I suppose it's a bit like what I have said regarding magic – you get out of it what you put into it!

All sorts of changes have happened as a result of this, one being that we no longer mix so much with the immediate Pagan community in Cornwall and socialise with a much more diverse set of friends and acquaintances. We still maintain our connections with the Museum of Witchcraft and the Pagan Federation, but have become less visible and taken more of a back seat (not to mention a well-earned rest!) from most of our voluntary work within the community. I've also entered the weird and wonderful world of blogs (why use an ugly and awkward word like 'blog' – I wonder where it comes from?). Laetitia, my partner frustrated by my frequent moans and grumps about things, or what she called my 'Victoria Meldrew' moments, suggested that I write down my grievances instead. I've done as suggested and my blog address can be found at the end of this book or on our website.

Incidentally, I was one of the few people who had never watched the TV programme 'One Foot in the Grave' but Laetitia soon rectified that by getting a set of the series which I duly watched. I could relate so well to where the poor, benighted Victor Meldrew was coming from, that I could see why Laetitia found my grumps so amusing – most of the time!

One thing that hasn't changed at all, but in fact has increased, is my commitment to my village community. Although I may have withdrawn from the world of self employment and income tax returns, I have found it necessary to step out from the shadows magically speaking in order to address some issues that were happening locally. That's when we realised that the cunning craft is not something that you retire from and I now work alongside Laetitia when we give consultations. We play to our own individual strengths, as a result teamwork is very successful as we can bounce off one another and talk things through afterwards. This was something that I was rarely able in the past to indulge in due to the confidential nature of consultations, but now we can 'debrief' each other.

Although the last couple of years have been tough and contained some dark and stormy moments, because we have persevered, the 'silver lining' is at last beginning to shine through. Whatever happens in the future, one thing I know for sure is - I will always remain Wisewoman of Buryan until I die – and knowing me, I will probably haunt the place afterwards such is my passion for this unique village and this Land!

Other Mandrake Titles

Craft of the Untamed
-An inspired vision of Traditional Witchcraft
By Nicholaj de Mattos Frisvold
isbn 978-1-906958-39-8 £25
The Craft of the Untamed sets out to present the main
pillars of traditional witchcraft. Its premise is that a proper
tradition is defined as a timeless unity. Outwardly the
tradition bears a great diversity across different lands and
spirit. Traditional witchcraft is found in various sodalities
and groups across the world. Even so it is possible to
discern several harmonious, shared themes. These themes
are the land, the crossroads, death, night and the mountain
of Venus. It is witchcraft where a human and angelic blood
mingles to form a special pedigree that has shaped the
archetypical image of the witch.

Fire Child - The Life and Magic
of Maxine Sanders 'Witch Queen' By Maxine Sanders
ISBN 978-1869928-780, Paperback, £12.99/$26
In this long awaited autobiography, Maxine reflects on her life
and magical career. From her unusual and disturbing childhood,
to her partnership with Alex Sanders; her joys and sorrows, her
vocation and work as a Priestess of the Goddess, teacher and
spiritual catalyst. This is a memoir of an extraordinary life, by
a rare, courageous and inspiring woman. *Fire Child* is pure
magic. Don't miss it!

The Arcane Veil: Witchcraft and Occult Science from
the People of the Dark-ages to the People of Goda, of
the Clan of Tubal Cain.'
By Shani Oates: Author of *Tubelo's Green Fire*
Special hbk: isbn 978-1-906958-35-0
Paperback: isbn 978-1-906958-36-7
An investigation of magical beliefs and practises in England
since 600CE to the post-modern fall-out of the 21st
century, analysing in particular its influences and survival
strategies. Emphasis is placed on Christian , Heathen, and
Hermetic Praxis, with provocative , critical study of the
concepts of Lucifer, Witch-Blood,Sin-Eating and their
influences on modern Traditional Craft praxes.

Lightning Source UK Ltd.
Milton Keynes UK
UKHW021517280820
368983UK00005B/309

9 781906 958237